WARTON'S
ESSAY ON POPE

The University of North Carolina Press, Chapel Hill, N. C.; The Baker and Taylor Company, New York; Oxford University Press, London; Maruzen-Kabushiki-Kaisha, Tokyo; Edward Evans & Son, Ltd., Shanghai; D. B. Centen's Wetenschappelijke Boekhandel, Amsterdam.

AN ESSAY ON THE WRITINGS AND GENIUS OF POPE.

SATYRA QUIDEM TOTA NOSTRA EST: IN QUA PRIMUS INSIGNEM LAUDEM ADEPTUS EST LUCILIUS; QUI QUOSDAM ITA DEDITOS SIBI ADHUC HABET AMATORES, UT EUM, NON EJUSDEM MODO OPERIS AUTORIBUS, SED OMNIBUS POETIS PRÆFERRE, NON DUBITENT.

QUINTILIAN.

LONDON:
PRINTED FOR M. COOPER, AT THE GLOBE IN PATER-NOSTER ROW.
MDCCLVI.

Title-page of the first edition of Joseph Warton's "An Essay on . . . Pope," 1756.

JOSEPH WARTON'S ESSAY ON POPE

A HISTORY OF THE FIVE EDITIONS

BY

WILLIAM DARNALL MacCLINTOCK, M.A.

Professor Emeritus of English
The University of Chicago

CHAPEL HILL
THE UNIVERSITY OF NORTH CAROLINA PRESS
1933

COPYRIGHT, 1933, BY
THE UNIVERSITY OF NORTH CAROLINA PRESS

To

P. L. M.

*to whom this study owes endless acknowledgment
for sound and practical judgment and for generous
laughter at its long delay.*

FOREWORD

In the stately eighteenth-century phrase of Warton "it is necessary and respectful" to inform the reader that the studies at the base of this paper were begun a long while ago.

They go back ultimately to Professor A. S. Cook, who, when I was a student at Johns Hopkins in 1880, first taught me respect for exact scholarship, and who later when I was preparing to teach at the newly founded University of Chicago, introduced me to the new science of text criticism, then just coming in from Europe, analyzing with me in detail many new books he had just imported. During the spring and summer of 1892 I pursued my studies at the British Museum and Bodleian libraries. It was then that I came upon Warton's *Essay*. These studies in criticism were continued in London in 1894 and 1899. By this time I was deep in Warton's work and had given graduate courses in English criticism and eighteenth-century literature at Chicago.

In 1902, with the help of Porter Lander MacClintock, I read the five editions together, taking notes of all changes in successive editions. By 1907 the materials for a full critical edition of the *Essay* were complete and it was accepted by Professor Ker for the series on criticism in the Athenaeum Press Series of Ginn and Co., Boston. But in 1908 this series was abandoned and my materials left in my hands. It was clear that they would make a large and costly book, which few publishers would undertake, considering the necessarily small public who might buy it.

In 1909 I decided to publish only what is here printed. But this seemed to call for a more careful and extended treatment of the rather technical matters involved than the original plan had made. So I have been guilty of more of the scholar's infinite delay, adding notes when working in the Museum in 1914 and 1920 but more extensively in the autumn of 1927 and the spring of 1928.

My original plan included the history of the five editions, and an introduction on Warton's critical ideas and their place in eighteenth-century literature, together with a large body of notes on Warton's notes. I have here attempted only the first. I am glad to record here my thanks for the help of my friend, John James Welker, recently a graduate scholar in the University of Chicago, who checked my quotations and references.

W. D. MacClintock

Chicago, 1933

TABLE OF CONTENTS

                                                        PAGE

FOREWORD ix

I. WARTON'S *ESSAY ON POPE*: ORIGIN, SIGNIFICANCE, RECEPTION 3

    The *Essay* in Relation to Contemporary Taste—Origins of the *Essay*—Matters Affecting Publication—The Title—The Dedication to Edward Young—Delay in Proceeding with Volume II—Translation into German—The Appendices—Reviews of the *Essay*—Warton's Edition of Pope's Works and Its Relation to the *Essay*.

II. A HISTORY OF THE FIVE EDITIONS................ 34

    The Value of Such a Study—The First Edition, 1756—The Second Edition, 1762—The Pirated Dublin Edition, 1764—The Third Edition, 1772—The Fourth Edition and the Second Volume, 1782—The Fifth Edition, 1806.

III. SUMMARY OF THE CHANGES MADE IN THE FIVE EDITIONS 43

    Technical and Bookish Changes—Changes Resulting from Growth in Taste and Judgment.

APPENDICES 71

    Biographical Note on Joseph Warton—A List of Warton's Literary Works—A Bibliographical Note.

LIST OF ILLUSTRATIONS

                                                                             PAGE

TITLE-PAGE OF THE FIRST EDITION OF JOSEPH WARTON'S
    An Essay on . . . Pope, 1756.....................Frontispiece

TITLE-PAGE OF THE SECOND EDITION, FIRST ISSUE, 1762......... 9

TITLE-PAGE OF THE SECOND EDITION, SECOND ISSUE, 1762........ 17

TITLE-PAGE OF THE PIRATED DUBLIN EDITION, 1764............ 23

TITLE-PAGE OF THE THIRD EDITION, 1772.................... 31

TITLE-PAGE OF THE FIRST ISSUE OF VOLUME II, 1782........... 39

TITLE-PAGE OF THE FOURTH EDITION OF VOLUME I, 1782........ 51

TITLE-PAGE OF VOLUME II (SECOND ISSUE), AS PART OF THE
    FOURTH EDITION OF THE COMPLETE ESSAY, 1782............ 55

TITLE-PAGE OF THE FIFTH EDITION, VOLUME I, 1806........... 63

TITLE-PAGE OF THE FIFTH EDITION, VOLUME II, 1806......... 67

WARTON'S
ESSAY ON POPE

I

THE *ESSAY ON POPE:* ORIGIN, SIGNIFICANCE, RECEPTION

The *Essay* in Relation to Contemporary Taste

HISTORIANS of culture agree that an actual revolution in taste took place when pleasure in the polished, moralizing couplets of Dryden, Pope, and Johnson gave place to enthusiasm for the freedom, individuality, strong emotion, and imagination of the romantic poets. To realize the contributions of both the classical and the romantic schools to the education of taste is to obtain a complete view of eighteenth-century poetry. Particularly important is the thorough study of the transition writers of the middle of the century, observing when they gradually break with the older order and begin feeling their way to new artistic principles. If students must choose among the many critics of the second and third quarters of the century, they should certainly select as guides Gray, Hurd, Lowth, and the Warton brothers.[1]

Among the critical studies that cannot be neglected is Joseph Warton's *Essay on the Genius and Writings of Pope*. It seems to me that this *Essay*, more completely than any other single piece of writing, expresses the period's consciousness of the faults in the writings of the Age of Queen Anne and the merits of the new work then appearing. Much of the *Essay* is in praise of Pope; much of it is timid and commonplace; but it must not be forgotten that so good a student of Pope as

[1] T. Warton, *Observations on the Faerie Queene of Spenser*, 1754; J. Warton, *Essay on Pope*, 1756; Richard Hurd, *Letters on Chivalry and Romance*, 1762; Bishop Thomas Percy, *Reliques of Ancient English Poetry* . . ., 1765; Thomas Gray's poems, letters, and criticism, from 1742 to 1775; Bishop Robert Lowth, *De Sacra Poesi Hebraeorum, Praelectiones Academicae Oxonii Habitae* . . ., 1753; T. Warton, *A History of English Poetry*, 1774-1781.

Mark Pattison affirms (in 1872) that Warton's notes on Pope's poems are still the best literary comment on them.[2] Of course Pattison is here thinking of Warton's edition of Pope's works in 1797, but he adds that the *Essay* is filled with those new notions concerning the imagination, nature, the sublime and pathetic, and exact imagery which he regards as so important in eighteenth-century criticism.

When the *Essay* appeared in 1756, it made a decided impression—indeed, it almost created a sensation. It challenged the supremacy of Pope, whose reputation was still high. We shall see elsewhere that it was widely read and that the second volume was eagerly awaited. It carried Warton's reputation forward to 1797 and helped to make a success of his edition of Pope's works.

When the Romantic Movement declined, however, the *Essay* began to lose influence. It seemed to the new age that finding fault with Pope was too much like beating a dead lion. In the first systematic history of English criticism[3] it is not even mentioned, the whole period from Pope to Wordsworth being given to Johnson. Saintsbury was the first unequivocally to give Warton the place he now holds.[4] So capable a critic as Professor Ker failed to appreciate Warton. Ker says concerning Dryden, "In a time when literature was pestered and cramped with formulas he found it impossible to write otherwise than freely. He is skeptical, tentative, disengaged, where most of his contemporaries, and most of his successors for a hundred years, are pledged to certain dogmas and principles."[5]

[2] Mark Pattison, *Essays* (ed. Henry Nettleship. 2 vols., Oxford, 1889), II, 368 ff.
[3] *English Literary Criticism* (ed. Charles Edwyn Vaughan, "The Warwick Library," London and New York, [1896]).
[4] George Saintsbury, *A History of Criticism* (3 vols., New York, Edinburgh, and London, 1904), III, 66 ff.
[5] John Dryden, *Essays* (ed. William Paton Ker, 2 vols., Oxford, 1900), I, xv.

But Gray and the Wartons, within the "hundred years" after Dryden, were not, apparently, "pledged to certain dogmas and principles."

This is not the place for an exposition of Warton's critical views and services, though it would be helpful if we had a complete and orderly survey of him in his own words. His ideas are scattered through the two volumes of the *Essay*, but a summary of them would occupy only a small space. Most of his voluminous notes were written to give sources, illustrations, and explanations of Pope's lines. His illuminating critical passages are those giving reasons for condemning Pope's work, those approving contemporary verse, and those containing the occasional speculations and freer "sports" of his own mind.

ORIGINS OF THE *Essay*

Mark Pattison perpetuated the widespread gossip of the eighteenth century that Warton's notes on Pope were called forth by Warburton's "polemical commentary" on Pope, not to answer it, but to show the proper way of annotating a classic.[6] Pattison is here speaking of Warton's edition of Pope's works in 1797, and not of the *Essay*, but we must bear in mind that all the valuable parts of the *Essay* were incorporated in the notes on Pope, which therefore look back to the origin of the *Essay*. This use of his *Essay* by Warton led, as we shall see, to the charge by current reviewers of his edition of Pope, that he was guilty of lazy and shabby work.[7]

That Warton was convinced of Warburton's errors as an editor may be seen in the Advertisement to his Pope,[8] but the *Essay* itself had its origin in the conviction formed by Warton before 1750 that Pope was not one of the greatest English poets. Perhaps the germ of the *Essay* may be found in pub-

---
[6] *Essays*, II, 368.   [7] See below, pp. 29-33.
[8] (9 vols., London, 1797), I, v. See John Wooll, *Biographical Memoirs of the Late Rev. Joseph Warton, D.D.* . . . (London, 1806), pp. 80 f.

lished form in Warton's *Ranelagh House* (1744).[9] This is a satire imitating Le Sage's *Le Diable Boiteux* (1707).[10] Ranelagh House is "the temple of Luxury, the theatre of Madness, the habitation of Folly."[11] Paraphrasing the poem, Wooll says, "the familiar spirit communicates to Philomides . . . that 'Mr. Pope had taken his place in the Elysian fields, not amongst the poets, but the philosophers; and that he was more fond of Socrates' company than Homer's.' "[12] Wooll therefore thinks that Warton's central idea as to the genius and place of Pope came to him very early. It will be recalled that Warton was only twenty-two years old when Pope died and this satire was published.

Further light is thrown on the origins of the *Essay* by Warton's Advertisement to his first published work, his *Odes on Various Subjects* (1746). Here he writes:

> The public has been so much accustomed of late to Didactic Poetry alone and Essays on moral subjects that any work where the Imagination is much indulged will perhaps not be relished or regarded. The author therefore of these pieces is in some pain lest certain austere critics should think these too fanciful and descriptive. But he is convinced that the fashion of moralizing in verse has been carried too far, and, as he looks upon Invention and Imagination to be the chief faculties of a Poet, so he will be happy if the following Odes may be looked upon as an attempt to bring back Poetry into its right channel.[13]

It should be recalled here, too, that in 1748 Warton and his sister published their father's poems, in which there was some poetry of a forward-looking character. This, together with his father's opinions, must have made a deep impression on the young critic's ideas. Then in 1754 his brother Thomas

---

[9] Reprinted by Wooll, *ibid.*, pp. 174-90.
[10] *Ibid.*, pp. 174, 176.   [11] *Ibid.*, p. 177.
[12] *Ibid.*, p. 35. The passage from Warton which Wooll gives here in direct quotation is also to be found with certain variations in his copy of the satire, p. 178 of the *Memoirs*.
[13] Preface to Warton's *Odes on Various Subjects* (1746), p. i.

ORIGIN, SIGNIFICANCE, RECEPTION 7

issued the *Observations on the Faerie Queene of Spenser*, written from the new "historical" point of view.[14] Joseph was deeply interested in Thomas's books, for the two brothers were close intellectual companions. Wooll says that Thomas helped with Joseph's edition of Virgil and in return was furnished with "many valuable materials for the History of English poetry."[15] After Thomas died in 1790, Joseph was employed by the publishers to finish the last volume of the *History* left by his brother but not quite complete, "though the ground I am to go over is so beaten."[16] Many passages in the *Essay* reflect the century's passion for Spenser and more than one author's awareness of "historical criticism."[17]

Another factor in the formation of Warton's critical views was his work on Virgil, mentioned above. On March 7, 1749/50, Warton agreed with Robert Dodsley to translate and edit the poems of Virgil, to furnish the copy within fifteen months, and to receive for his labor £200 and a few perquisites; he gave a receipt on November 15, 1752, for £221.[18] The work appeared in four volumes in June, 1753.[19] This undertaking forced him to determine closely his ideas as to

[14] C. Rinaker, *Thomas Warton, a Biographical and Critical Study* (University of Illinois Studies in Language and Literature, II [1916], 1-241.

[15] Wooll, *Memoirs*, p. 75.   [16] *Ibid.*, p. 404.

[17] See 1 (1st ed.), pp. 32 ff., 247 n. See also below, pp. 35, 64, 66. Warton was a close friend of James Harris (1709-1780), who wrote three important books dealing with the principles and history of criticism. They were all published by his son James in 1801, though they had all appeared earlier—the first in 1744, the second in 1751, and the third in 1781. Warton cites the *Discourse on Music, Painting*, etc., in his first edition (1756), p. 178, as "the genuine method of criticising," and refers to it four times in his 4th ed. (1782): I, 179; II, 80, 86, 92. Harris's *Hermes* he quotes at length in 1756 (*Essay*, p. 120 n. The *Philological Enquiries* (three parts, 1781) he does not use, but since it was worked up from a sketch made in 1752, he must have known its author's very significant ideas as to the history and types of criticism. The section on "Historical Criticism," with its long list of critics for examples, influenced Warton greatly *me judice*.

[18] Ralph Straus, *Robert Dodsley* (London and New York, [1910]), p. 346 Straus gives full text of agreement.

[19] *The Works of Virgil in Latin and English* (London). Wooll, p. 20.

pastoral, didactic, and epic poetry, on which themes he wrote introductory essays.

But the most convincing evidence of Warton's attitude toward Pope and of the critical views that produced the *Essay* is to be found in his Dedicatory Letter to Edward Young, in the first edition. He says:

> No love of singularity, no affectation of paradoxical opinions, gave rise to the following Work. I revere the memory of Pope, I respect and honour his abilities; but I do not think him at the head of his profession. In other words, in the species of poetry wherein Pope excelled, he is superior to all mankind: and I only say, that this species of poetry is not the most excellent one of the art. We do not, it would seem, sufficiently attend to the difference there is, betwixt a MAN OF WIT, a MAN OF SENSE, and a TRUE POET. Donne and Swift, were undoubtedly men of wit and men of sense: but what traces have they left of PURE POETRY?[20]

Warton probably owed this distinction between a man of sense in art and a true poet to Dryden, who, in his dedication to *Eleanora* first said that Donne was a man of wit but not the best of poets.[21] Pope had said practically the same thing, that "Donne had no imagination, but as much wit, I think, as any writer can possibly have."[22]

Warton continues:

> Fontenelle and La Motte are entitled to the former character; but what can they urge to gain the latter? Which of these characters is the most valuable and useful, is entirely out of the question; all I plead for, is, to have their several provinces kept distinct from each other; and to impress on the reader, that a clear head, and acute understanding, are not sufficient, alone, to make a POET; that the most solid observations on human life, expressed with the utmost elegance and brevity, are MORALITY, and not POETRY; that the EPISTLES of

---

[20] I (1756), iii ff.
[21] Dryden's *Works* (Edinburgh, 1882-93), XI, 123.
[22] Joseph Spence, *Anecdotes, Observations, and Characters, of Books and Men* . . . (ed. Samuel Weller Singer, London and Edinburgh, 1820), p. 136.

AN ESSAY ON THE GENIUS AND WRITINGS OF POPE.

THE SECOND EDITION,
CORRECTED AND ENLARGED.

SATYRA QUIDEM TOTA NOSTRA EST: IN QUA PRIMUS INSIGNEM LAUDEM ADEPTUS EST LUCILIUS; QUI QUOSDAM ITA DEDITOS SIBI ADHUC HABET AMATORES, UT EUM, NON EJUSDEM MODO OPERIS AUTORIBUS, SED OMNIBUS POETIS PRÆFERRE, NON DUBITENT.
QUINTILIAN.

LONDON:

PRINTED FOR M. COOPER, AT THE GLOBE IN PATER-NOSTER ROW.

Title-page of the second edition (first issue) of Joseph Warton's "An Essay on . . . Pope," 1762.

Boileau in RHYME, are no more poetical, than the CHARACTERS of Bruyère in PROSE; and that it is a creative and glowing IMAGINATION, "acer spiritus ac vis," and that alone, that can stamp a writer with this exalted and very uncommon character, which so few possess, and of which so few can properly judge.[23]

So much for the remoter origins of the *Essay*. Its more immediate inspiration may be found, I think, in Warton's relation with Joseph Spence (1699-1768). It is well known that Warton was greatly indebted to Spence for anecdotes and personal impressions of Pope; it should be equally clear that he owed to him much of his philosophy of poetry, or, if he did not actually owe Spence this debt, that the two critics were pursuing the same lines of thought.

In 1726 and 1727 Spence published *An Essay on Pope's Odyssey*, which is, on the whole, a fulsome eulogy but which contains also many notes on Pope's weaknesses and some new general ideas as to poetry and taste. One particular passage in this essay influenced Warton greatly. Spence says, "With Poets and in History, *there may be some Fraud in saying only the bare truth.* In either, 'tis not sufficient to tell us, that *such a City*, for Instance, *was taken and ravag'd with a great deal of Inhumanity:* There is a *Poetical Falsity*, if a strong Idea of each particular be not imprinted on the mind; and an *Historical*, if some things are passed over only with a general mark of Infamy or Dislike."[24] Spence adds, "It was in *Quintilian* I first met with this Observation," and cites the *De institutione oratoria*, Lib. viii. cap. 3.

In 1726 also Spence began collecting the famous *Anecdotes, Observations, and Characters, of Books and Men,* continuing them till 1744 and adding later supplements from his notes and memoranda books up to 1758. Though many critics and

---

[23] *Essay on Pope* (1756), I, iii ff.
[24] (London and Oxford, 1726-27), Part II (1727), 121 f.

ORIGIN, SIGNIFICANCE, RECEPTION 11

biographers of the eighteenth century had the use of this collection, it was not published until 1820, when Malone and Singer brought it out almost simultaneously. In 1728 Spence succeeded Warton's father as professor of poetry at Oxford.

In the *Gentleman's Magazine* for May, 1782, a reviewer says that Pope would have approved of Warton's *Essay* and that it "owes much of its embellishment also to the manuscript remarks of Mr. Spence, communicated to the author on a visit at Byfleet in 1752."[25] It would appear either that there was more than one visit about this time, or that the date 1752 is wrong. Otherwise Wooll could not have remarked that Warton had praised the moderns as he had already done the ancients,[26] for Warton's edition of Virgil appeared in 1753.

We recall that Warburton's first edition of Pope appeared in quarto form in 1743, and his second in octavo in 1752, with notes full of highly controversial theological matter.[27] Warton, it seems certain, wished to produce, in his *Essay*, a book of strictly literary comment, as well as to express his conviction, formed earlier as I have shown, that Pope was not one of our greatest poets. Everything points to the fact that it was Warburton's editions of Pope that set Warton to work on his *Essay*. As to the visits to Spence, one is dated by Warton himself. In Volume II of the *Essay* (1782), he says that he is indebted to

[25] *Gentleman's Magazine: and Historical Chronicle*, LII, 240.
[26] Wooll, p. 30. See p. 12 below.
[27] In his first edition of 1756, p. 136, commenting on ll. 150 f., of Pope's *Essay on Criticism*, Warton says, "Here is evidently a blameable mixture of metaphors; where the attributes of the horse and the writer are confounded." But a certain "Adurfi," in a letter to the *Gentleman's Magazine*, August 1, 1781 (LI, 366), points out that it was Warburton who made the mixture by shuffling Pope's lines and cites the earlier edition for proof. Then the next year, in his much corrected and final fourth edition of the *Essay*, Warton makes a note on p. 136, vol. I, saying, "These lines were thus printed in Dr. Warburton's quarto edition, 1743; pg. 16: and again in the octavo edition made use of in this work, 1752." But on the next page he continues the charge, evidently not using some of the explanation in the *Gentleman's Magazine* of the year before.

Mr. Spence "for most of the anecdotes relating to *Pope* . . . which he gave me when I was making him a visit at Byfleet, in the year 1754."[28] On November 2, 1754, Spence wrote to Thomas Warton, Jr., "As my summer has been so much taken up, if this place [Byfleet] should lie at all in the way of you or your brother, or rather both, it would be a kind and charitable thing to look in upon one in the winter."[29]

Whatever the dates of these visits, Wooll is justified in saying that it was under Spence's roof that Warton "laid the foundation of those critical disquisitions which proved his competency of deciding on the merits of modern, as his Virgil had done on those of ancient poetry."[30]

MATTERS AFFECTING THE PUBLICATION OF THE *Essay*

The Publishers.—The famous publishers Robert and James Dodsley were close friends of Joseph Warton; he corresponded with Robert regularly and visited him when in town. But when the first edition of the *Essay* appeared in 1756, no publisher was given. The only information given is that it was "Printed for M. Cooper, at the Globe in Pater-noster Row." "M. Cooper," Mary Cooper, was the widow of Thomas Cooper,[31] a publisher who printed books for Dodsley and who sold or circulated them from his own shops. Most of Dodsley's books were printed by John Hughs,[32] who was another of these printer-publishers; it was from his press, Timperley tells us, that "almost the whole of the numerous and valuable publications of the Dodsley's" were issued.[33]

---

[28] II (4th ed.), 239.
[29] Wooll, pp. 226 f. [30] *Ibid.*, p. 30.
[31] "Yesterday died Thomas Cooper, publisher, 2 Pater-noster Row . . ."—London *Evening Post*, Feb. 10, 1743.
[32] John Nichols, *Literary Anecdotes of the Eighteenth Century* (9 vols., London, 1812-15), VIII (1814), 403.
[33] Charles Henry Timperley, *A Dictionary of Printers and Printing*, . . . (London, Edinburgh, Glasgow, Dublin, and Manchester, 1839), p. 726.

ORIGIN, SIGNIFICANCE, RECEPTION 13

But though Mrs. Cooper appears as the ostensible publisher, Robert Dodsley actually supervised closely its appearance. His name was omitted from the title-page for a reason given by him in a letter to Warton, April 8, 1756.[34] This reason was, in general, that he could push the sale of the book more vigorously and comment on it more freely if his name were not attached to it. Mrs. Cooper, who continued her husband's business after his death in 1743, died in 1761, and the Dodsley name appears for the first time on the title-page of Warton's *Essay* in its second edition late in 1762. There is nothing unusual in Dodsley's name's having been omitted from the first edition, for the practice of using some other name as a shield was a common one among the publishers of the eighteenth century.

Circulation of the Essay.—It is clear from the book catalogues issued from 1762 to 1811,[35] as well as from the advertising sections of the chief magazines of the day, that Warton's

[34] Wooll, p. 237. See pp. 36-37 below.
[35] A list of the more important catalogues follows:
  1. 1762.—A list of books published by Dodsley, given in Straus's *Robert Dodsley*, p. 376. Here for the first time, Jan. 22, 1762, occurs a notice of the *Essay* in the book catalogues.
  2. 1764.—*Catalogue . . . of books . . . published these sixty years past.* The *Essay* is not listed under Warton, whose name did not appear on the title-page till 1782, but merely as *An Essay*, etc.
  3. 1766.—*A Complete Catalogue of Modern Books, 1700-1766.*
  4. 1767.—*A New and Corrected Catalogue of All English Books from 1706 . . .*
  5. 1775.—*The London Catalogue of Books since 1700.*
  6. 1779.—*A General Catalogue of Books . . . 1700 to the Present Time.*
  7. 1786.—*A General Catalogue of Books in All Languages, Arts, and Sciences, printed in Great Britain and published in London from the year MDCC to MDCCLXXXVI.* This gives both the Vol. I and the Vols. I and II issued 1756 and 1782.
  8. 1788.—*A Modern Catalogue of Books.*
  9. 1791.—*The London Catalogue of Books.* This was No. 7, selected and enlarged.
  10. 1811.—*The London Catalogue of Books . . .* , corrected to August, 1811.

Essay was well advertised. The size of the volumes was regularly octavo and the price five or six shillings a volume except for one handsome edition in 1811, after Warton's death.

Compensation to the Author.—In 1774, when the agitation against perpetual copyright was intense,[36] the publishers laid before Parliament two lists. One was to show printed books with abundant copies in stock, giving the prices and the number of years they had been on sale. This was to show that there was no monopoly causing shortage of books. The other list was to show that the authors were paid liberally for their work especially for revisions and new editions. For example, Johnson was paid £300 for his third edition of Dryden's *Works*. Editions of Shakespeare were paid for as follows: Pope, £217; Theobald, £652; Warburton, £500; Capell, £300; and Johnson, £475. I have not found what Warton was paid for the editions of his *Essay*, but for his edition of Virgil in 1753 he received £221,[37] and for his edition of Pope's *Works*, £500.[38]

Piracies.—Piracies of English books were frequent in Ireland and occasional in Scotland. In a letter to Edward Mills, August 7, 1758, Goldsmith says, "Every work published here [London] the printers in Ireland republish there, without giving the author the least consideration for his copy."[39] Ireland did not come under the copyright law until the Act of Union, January 1, 1801. A Dublin reprint of Warton's *Essay* appeared in 1764, published by Peter Wilson, Dame Street. It is boldly called on the title-page the "Third Edition." This of course

---

[36] See W. A. Copinger, *On the Law of Copyright* . . . (ed. James, London, 1927), pp. 9 f.; A. S. Collins, *Authorship in the Days of Johnson* (London, 1927), pp. 8 f., 64-68, 71, 101; A. W. Pollard, "Notes on the History of Copyright in England, 1662-1774," *The Library*, Fourth Series, III (Sept., 1922), 97-114 (*Transactions of the Bibliographical Society*, Second Series, Vol. III (1922).

[37] See p. 7 above.   [38] See pp. 29-33 below.

[39] *Works* (ed. Peter Cunningham, New York, 1881), IV, 485. Cf. *ibid.*, p. 491. See also Goldsmith, *Collected Letters* (ed. Katherine C. Balderston, Cambridge, 1928), p. 34.

is false. The legitimate third edition appeared in London in 1772.

As to these piracies, Pollard thinks the act of 1709 was essentially successful and that "pirated reprints did not appear in book-seller's shops" in London, though they may have been for sale in the streets or in the country.[40] He traces the history of the piracies as due to the increased prices in 1711 of print paper and of unfinished books. Irish printers, he says, because of the lower duties in Ireland, reprinted English books and sent them to England.

Prices.—Between 1700 and 1756, according to Knight,[41] the price of octavo volumes, in which size Warton's *Essay* was published through every edition, was five or six shillings. I find no notice of more or less costly issues. Knight adds that by 1800 this price was increased 50 to 100 per cent, and that new books were issued for an "exclusive market," that is, for a select group of readers. The popular market was supplied by cheap issues of old books and by circulating libraries.

Size of Editions.—I have found no statement by Warton or his publishers as to the size of the editions of the *Essay*. The following notes are, I hope, pertinent. Of Thomas Warton's *Observations on the Faerie Queene of Spenser* (1754), a book very like his brother's *Essay on Pope* and published by the same publishers, five hundred copies were first issued.[42] Hume thought fifteen hundred copies large for an edition of his "philosophic pieces."[43] Gibbon said of his *History of the Decline and Fall of the Roman Empire,* "So moderate were our hopes, that the original impression had been stinted to five hun-

---

[40] *Op. cit.*, p. 111.
[41] Charles Knight, *Shadows of the Old Booksellers* (London, 1865), pp. 311-13.
[42] Wooll, p. 220.
[43] David Hume to his publisher, William Strahan, 25 March, 1774.—*Letters of David Hume* (ed. G. B. Hill, 1888).

dred, till the number was doubled by the prophetic taste of Mr. Strahan."[44] On May 25, 1777, Strahan wrote as to the first edition, "The [second] impression is to be fifteen hundred and no more, which is of all others the most proper number."[45] So a thousand copies were printed of the first edition and fifteen hundred of the second, which, according to Gibbon, were "moving off with decent speed," and a third edition was threatened for the next year.[46] Each of the ten editions of the *Rambler* during Johnson's lifetime, says Hill, following Hawkins, was of twelve hundred and fifty copies.[47]

Estimating cautiously from these figures, I judge that between four and five thousand copies of the *Essay* must have been printed during Warton's lifetime.

THE TITLE OF THE *Essay*

The first edition of the first volume of the *Essay* has the title thus: *An Essay on the Writings and Genius of Pope*. All the other editions of either Volume I or Volume II change the title to *An Essay on the Genius and Writings of Pope*, except that the first printing of Volume II in 1782, part of which is said to have been printed before 1762, has the original order in the running head. This shows that the printed sheets so long withheld from publication were used in the first issue early in 1782.[48]

THE DEDICATION TO EDWARD YOUNG

In a dedicatory letter[49] to Dr. Edward Young, rector of Welwyn, partly personal but chiefly critical and even polemical,

---

[44] Quoted from Knight, *Shadows of the Old Booksellers*, p. 226.
[45] A. S. Collins, *Authorship in the Days of Johnson* (London, 1927), p. 198.
[46] Knight, *op. cit.*, p. 227.
[47] Boswell's *Life of Johnson* (ed. G. B. Hill), I, 246, n. 2. Hill cites Hawkins' *Life of Johnson*, p. 269.
[48] See p. 21 below.
[49] This was not signed in any edition during Warton's life and was not dated until the third edition of 1772.

AN ESSAY
ON THE
GENIUS
AND
WRITINGS
OF
POPE.

The SECOND EDITION, Corrected.

Satyra quidem tota nostra est: in qua primus insignem laudem adeptus est Lucilius; qui quosdam ita deditos sibi adhuc habet amatores, ut eum, non ejusdem modo operis autoribus, sed omnibus poetis, præferre non dubitent.   QUINTILIAN.

LONDON,
PRINTED FOR R. AND J. DODSLEY, IN PALL-MALL.
MDCCLXII.

Title-page of the second edition (second issue) of Joseph Warton's "An Essay on . . . Pope," 1762.

Warton really writes a preface to his *Essay*. This dedication, together with Young's *Conjectures on Original Composition* (1759), shows that the two critics had the same opinions as to Pope, especially as to his being a man of wit rather than a true poet. The core or thesis of the *Essay* is the principle that if a writer has the natural gift of moral or satirical poetry, he "will never succeed, with equal merit, in the higher branches of his art."[50] Young and Warton must have exchanged opinions for years, and since the former was much the older man (born in 1683), he may have been the originator of many of the ideas they shared.

At the end of the dedication Warton gives a classification of English poets, making four groups:[51]

1. "Sublime and pathetic poets: Spenser, Shakespeare, Milton; and then, at proper intervals, Otway and Lee."

2. "Such as possessed the true poetical genius, in a more moderate degree, but had noble talents for moral and ethical poesy. At the head of these are Dryden, Donne, Denham, Cowley, Congreve."

3. Here are placed "men of wit, of elegant taste, and some fancy in describing familiar life." Warton mentions here Prior, Waller, Parnell, Swift, and Fenton.

4. The fourth class includes "mere versifiers," such as Pitt, Sandys, Fairfax, Broome, Buckingham, and Lansdowne. He concludes, "in which of these classes POPE deserves to be placed, the following Work is intended to determine."

In the second edition of the *Essay* (1762), this classification is much altered. Otway and Lee are dropped entirely from their dizzy height, Addison is added to the second class, and several are raised to it from the original third class. To the third are added one (Donne) from above, and several from the wide world. The fourth class remains unchanged. Evidently War-

[50] See I (5th ed.), 65.   [51] I (1st ed.), xi f.

ORIGIN, SIGNIFICANCE, RECEPTION 19

ton had heard from his friends and enemies and hastened to save himself. He apologizes by saying, "This enumeration is not intended as a complete catalogue, . . . but only to mark out briefly the different species of our celebrated authors."[52] As an influential document in the history of the Romantic Movement, this dedication deserves the attention scholars have long given it. Students who may be interested in this classification and ordering of our poets, attempted by many eighteenth-century critics, may profitably consult *The Literary Review* for January, 1758,[53] where an anonymous writer not only lists all English poets, but gives the "points" on which he classifies them. One is glad to see that Chaucer is here well placed, though below Pope and Cowley, while Pope is placed at the head.

WARTON'S DELAY IN PROCEEDING WITH VOLUME II

It is clear that after the publication of Volume I in 1756, Warton actively worked at Volume II. While we have little direct evidence of these activities, indirectly we know much. At the time he was working on Volume II, he tells us later, there was no translation of Sophocles in English.[54] He must have meant no translation in verse, for G. Adams had published his *Tragedies of Sophocles translated* [in prose] *from the Greek*, in 1729. Now Thomas Francklin published his *Tragedies of Sophocles translated* [in verse] *from the Greek*, in 1759. This particular passage, then, was written before 1759. Section VII of the *Essay*, in which this note appears, was early in 1782, at the beginning of the second volume (first edition of Volume II), but was moved back to Volume I, for the sake of uniform size, when the whole *Essay* was reprinted later in the same year. The passage to which this note is appended is

[52] I (2nd ed.), xii.   [53] III, 6.
[54] I (4th ed.), 379 n.—"When this was written the tragedies of Sophocles, Aeschylus, and Euripides, had not been translated."

on page 30 of the first edition of Volume II, and hence belongs to that part of the book printed "above twenty years ago," as Warton says in the Advertisement to the first edition of this volume.[55] Again, he mentions Mason's *Caractacus* as "recent."[56] This appeared in 1759 and helps to date the writing of Volume II.

That he would proceed with Volume II was expected by his close friends. For instance, on April 6, 1769, after the appearance of Ruffhead's *Life of Pope*, Dr. Thomas Balguy writes to Warton urging him to ignore "this wretched biographer" and saying that all he deserves is thanks "for the occasion he gives you of printing your second volume."[57] On April 19, 1759, Dr. Lowth writes, "I was very glad to see that you were fairly engaged in the 2d volume; and hope you will go on with it with alacrity and expedition."[58]

The question, then, as to why Warton did not proceed with the publication of the second volume of the *Essay* is a very interesting one.[59] We have little direct information. The delay was long supposed to be due to Warton's "fear" of the wrath of Warburton, who had edited Pope's works in 1751 and was jealous of any attack on Pope. Warburton was a close friend of Warton's brother Thomas. He had furnished Ruffhead the materials for his lumbering *Life of Pope* (1769), which was a kind of reply to Warton's *Essay*.[60] Johnson

[55] II (1st ed.), i. [57] Wooll, pp. 343 ff.
[56] I (4th ed.), 69 n. [58] *Ibid.*, p. 261.
[59] That he was at work at it is shown in a footnote (II [1st ed.], 256), where he says, "The chapel of New College in Oxford will soon receive a singular and invaluable ornament: A window, the glass of which is stained by Mr. Jervis, from that exquisite picture of the Nativity by Sir Joshua Reynolds." The window was installed in 1777, and Thomas Warton in 1782 published "Verses on Sir Joshua Reynolds's Painted Window at New-College, Oxford."
[60] See Alexander Chalmers, "The Life of Dr. Joseph Warton," in *The Works of the English Poets, from Chaucer to Cowper* . . . , ed. Chalmers, (London, Cambridge, and York, 1810), XVIII, 151.

ORIGIN, SIGNIFICANCE, RECEPTION

mentioned the two works in a conversation (March 31, 1772) worth quoting here in full:

He censured Ruffhead's *Life of Pope;*[61] and said, "he knew nothing of Pope, and nothing of poetry." He praised Dr. Joseph Warton's *Essay on Pope;* but said, he supposed we should have no more of it, as the authour had not been able to persuade the world to think of Pope as he did. BOSWELL. "Why, Sir, should that prevent him from continuing his work? He is an ingenious Counsel, who has made the most of his cause: he is not obliged to gain it." JOHNSON. "But, Sir, there is a difference when the cause is of a man's own making."[62]

The foregoing quotations show that during the sixteen years following the publication of the *Essay,* there was talk among Warton's friends of his continuing it. Singer says that Warburton had taken all the valuable things in Ruffhead's *Life* from Spence, and without any acknowledgment; and that it was probably for this reason that Ruffhead's *Life of Pope* was not published until after Spence's death in 1768.[63] Chalmers suggests that Warton was partly afraid of Warburton and partly deferential toward him and was only waiting for Warburton's death to continue his second volume.[64] This opinion seems confirmed by the fact (which Chalmers mentions) that it was not until after Warburton died, in 1779, that Warton issued, in 1782, the long delayed second volume—which had been left half printed twenty years before. This view of Chalmers, as was pointed out above, was current in Warton's lifetime and has persisted since. Wooll merely says that War-

[61] Johnson said of Ruffhead (I am quoting from G. B. Hill's edition of Boswell, II, 166 f., n. 4): "'Mr. Ruffhead says of fine passages, that they are fine, and of feeble passages, that they are feeble; but recommending poetical beauty, is like remarking the splendour of sunshine; to those who can see, it is unnecessary, and to those who are blind, absurd.' *Gent. Mag.,* Vol. XXXIX, May, 1769, p. 255. The review in which this passage occurs, is perhaps in part Johnson's."

[62] Boswell's *Life of Johnson* (ed. G. B. Hill), II, 166 f.
[63] Spence, *Anecdotes* (ed. S. W. Singer), pp. ix f.
[64] *Op. cit.,* XVIII, 151.

ton's delay was due to "motives of a most delicate and laudable nature."[65] As late as 1915 Gosse said that the *Essay* "was so shocking to the prejudices of the hour that it was received with universal disfavor, and twenty-six years passed before the author had the moral courage to pursue it to a conclusion."[66] My notes on the reviews of the *Essay* show this opinion to be largely erroneous.[67]

It seems to me that this theory of Warton's fearing Warburton's wrath is only partly true. In 1762 he issued a second, revised and strengthened, edition of Volume I, which contained his most radical assertions, and in 1772, a third and further strengthened edition. Evidently Warton was for two decades not "afraid" of offending the powerful and ill-natured bishop. I am convinced that the reasons for the delay must be found in his absorption in school work, in his natural sluggishness, and especially in his lack of interest in the poems of Pope to be treated in this volume. These were the poems which required the largest amount of illustrative material from the classics, and for whose treatment there was need of extensive reading. It was also the part of Pope's poetry less easily illustrated from recent literary and critical work. It is possible that Warton wrote all of the matter for Volume II before 1762, though I think it unlikely. He did print two hundred pages of it and then stopped. Later, when this portion was reissued, in 1782, he made two hundred and thirty-one changes in it.

Translation into German

The translation of the *Essay* into German is found in *Sammlung vermischter Schriften zur Beförderung der schönen Wissenschaften und der freyen Künste. Des sechsten Bandes, erstes und zweites Stück*, Berlin, Friedrich Nicolai, 1763. Pub-

---
[65] P. 55.
[66] Edmund Gosse, *Two Pioneers of Romanticism: Joseph and Thomas Warton*, Proceedings of the British Academy, 1915-1916, p. 157.
[67] See below, pp. 24-29.

AN ESSAY ON THE GENIUS AND WRITINGS OF POPE.

THE THIRD EDITION,
CORRECTED AND ENLARGED.

Satyra quidem tota noſtra eſt: in qua primus inſignem laudem adeptus eſt Lucilius; qui quoſdam ita deditos ſibi adhuc habet amatores, ut eum, non ejuſdem modo operis autoribus, ſed omnibus poetis præferre, non dubitent. QUINTILIAN.

DUBLIN:
Printed for PETER WILSON, in *Dame-ſtreet.*
MDCCLXIV.

Title-page of the pirated Dublin edition of Joseph Warton's "An Essay on ... Pope," 1764.

lication of this miscellany of books and articles was begun in 1759. There are in the British Museum six numbers, dated respectively 1759 (two numbers), 1760, 1761, 1762, and 1763. They are now bound in two volumes. There is no indication of editor or translator. The translation of Warton's *Essay* occupies all of the sixth number, of three hundred pages, and is in two parts or sections. All passages from Pope are translated. Number II, now Volume I, pages 206-219, contains Edward Young's *Abhändlung über die Lyrische Dichtkunst*. (Aus dem Englischen übersetzt.)

The Appendices

To the fourth edition in 1782 Warton added two appendices, one on the *Alma* of Prior,[68] and one giving a "Summary of the Arguments of each Scene and Act, in *L'Adamo* of G. B. Andreini."[69]

On February 6, 1792, he writes to his friend, John Wilkes, "If I had seen you before I left town, I would have informed you that I am sending up to the press an Appendix to my Essay on Pope, a pamphlet of about 130 pages.[70] I trust you may see in it some entertaining particulars. I find myself obliged frequently to contradict Johnson, as well as Warburton."[71] This would show that Warton planned another edition of the *Essay* for 1792. No such edition came out, and Wooll does not refer to this manuscript for another appendix.

Reviews of the *Essay*

The most important reviewing magazines in England between 1750 and 1780 were, in the order of their beginnings:

---

[68] Referred to, II, 126. [69] Referred to, II, 183.
[70] So in MS; 130 is impossible, and 13 was probably intended. Nichols (see following note), reads 13.
[71] John Wilkes, "Select Correspondence," XI (1754-1797), British Museum, Add. MSS. 30877, fol. 116. See also Nichols, *Literary Anecdotes*, IX (1815), 474.

ORIGIN, SIGNIFICANCE, RECEPTION

Gentleman's Magazine; or, Monthly Intelligencer, 1731.
London Magazine; or, Gentleman's Monthly Intelligencer, 1732.
Monthly Review, 1749.
Critical Review; or, Annals of Literature, 1756.
Literary Magazine, or, Universal Review, 1756.

Warton's *Essay*, Volume I, was announced as published in the *Gentleman's Magazine*, March, 1756. It was reviewed in the *Critical Review* in April, under the caption, "Art. V. An Essay on the Writings and Genius of Pope. 8°. Pr. 5s. M. Cooper."[72]

It is, on the whole, a sympathetic and sufficiently laudatory paper, though it does not get at Warton's main points, and it takes strong issue with Warton on many detailed matters. It quotes many pages and concludes that the *Essay* is "a work of taste and learning, animated with many strokes of manly criticism, replete with knowledge, and diversified with a number of amusing incidents and observations."[73] The review is unsigned, and Warton's name is not mentioned.

In the April-May, 1756, number of the *Literary Magazine*, Dr. Johnson reviewed the *Essay*, giving four pages of extract, exposition, and comment. The review is moderate, unenthusiastic, appreciative, and cleverly critical and levelheaded. Johnson's comments are about equally divided between agreement with and praise of Warton, on the one hand, and disagreement or objection, on the other. While some of his sentences have keen point, for the most part he merely quibbles or insists on a common-sense view of Pope's lines. Warton objects to *Windsor Forest* as filled with images not peculiar to the place but "equally applicable to any place whatsoever." Johnson says we must first "inquire whether Windsor Forest has in reality something peculiar." This misses

[72] I, 226-40. See p. 36.   [73] *Ibid.*, p. 240.

Warton's point entirely. Again, Warton says that unvaried rhymes disgust a reader who has a good ear. Johnson objects that it is "surely not the ear but the mind that is offended, the fault rising from the use of common rhymes is that in reading the first line the second may be guessed and half the composition loses the grace of writing." This seems like pure quibbling. On Warton's remarks as to *The Rape of the Lock*, Johnson says, "There is in his remarks on this work no discovery of any latent beauty, nor anything subtle or striking. Warton is indeed commonly right but has discussed no difficult question." Here the modern student feels that Johnson strikes home. Warton says of one of Pope's similes, "It is sufficiently obvious." Johnson remarks, "I do not remember that it is obvious—which is very easy to say and easy to deny. Many things are obvious when they are taught." Of Warton's criticisms of the *Epistle of Eloisa to Abelard*, Johnson writes that Warton "disposes many agreeable particulars and incidental relations, but there is not much profundity of criticism." This is sound and just.

In conclusion, Johnson says that he intends "to kindle, not to extinguish curiosity, by this slight sketch of a work abounding with various quotations and pleasing disquisitions," and that "most men find in it many things that they did not know before, and the learned may read the book as a just specimen of literary moderation." On the whole, the review is a cramped, mild, and rather cold approval by Johnson, with several distinct "digs" that could not have been pleasing to Warton. But so large a space given to the book, and even grudging praise from the great Johnson, were distinct gains for Warton's venture.

The volume was also reviewed in 1756 in the June and July numbers of the *Monthly Review*.[74] On the whole, the judgment is favorable, and the reviewer hopes the author will

[74] XIV (1756), 528-54; XV (1756), 52-78.

ORIGIN, SIGNIFICANCE, RECEPTION 27

"continue his Observations,"[75] a suggestion that may have a bearing on what Warton actually did. In the *London Magazine's* monthly catalogue of books for March and April, 1756, occurs the following: "41. An Essay on the Writings and Genius of Pope, pr. 5 s. Cooper."[76] This magazine did not further notice the *Essay*.

An "Epitome" of the *Essay*, given in some detail, appears in the "List of Books Published, with Remarks," in the May and June numbers of the *Gentleman's Magazine* of 1756.[77] The "remarks" are generally favorable and conclude with the paragraph:

> Upon the whole, this *Essay on the Writings and Genius of Pope* is a most entertaining and useful miscellany of literary knowledge and candid criticism, containing censure without acrimony, and praise without flattery; and abounding with incidents little known, relating to celebrated writers, and instructive remarks upon their characters and works.

I find no mention of the second edition of Volume I in 1762, or of the third edition in 1772, in either the *Gentleman's Magazine* or the *Monthly Review*, where especially we might have expected it. The *Critical Review* for May, 1782, has a short notice of an anonymous work, *An Historical and Critical Account of the Lives and Writings of the Living Authors of Great Britain*,[78] and in this notice the reviewer scorns the author for omitting to mention "some of the best writers of the age . . . ; such as Mr. Mallet, the two Wartons, Mr. Paul Whitehead, Mr. Cooper, Mr. Melmoth, Mr. Home, Dr. Robertson, Dr. Campbell, Mr. Guthrie, and many others."[79]

[75] *Ibid.*, XV, 78.
[76] The *London Magazine; or, Gentleman's Monthly Intelligencer*, XXV (1756), 199; the monthly catalogue (when published) was generally given for two months at a time. It was omitted from the March number; the citation is to the May number.
[77] XXVI (1756), 249-51, 305-6.
[78] XIII, 441. [79] *Ibid.*, p. 442.

Volume II of the *Essay*, which appeared in 1782, was reviewed in the *Gentleman's Magazine* for May.[80] The review is mostly a mere running account of Warton's work, with many quotations. The *Essay* is a "liberal and elegant piece of criticism," says the reviewer. "The IId [volume] has been impatiently expected; and some anachronisms in it are accounted for from the first 200 pages (there are 495 in all) having been 'printed above twenty years ago' "[81]—this last taken from Warton's Advertisement. In his summary the reviewer says that Warton has "Something to blame and something to commend" (quoting Pope), and that "almost every criticism is supported by scientific reasons."[81a] The reviewer also says that the *Essay* gives a review of most of the literary characters of the time, and that Pope would, no doubt, have approved of Warton's *Essay* as he did of that of Spence on his *Odyssey*.

The volume was also reviewed in the *Critical Review*, February, 1782.[82] The reviewer begins, "This work has long been expected, and even called for, by the public." We recall that the first volume was reviewed in this journal in 1756, and observations were made on it in an account of Ruffhead's *Life of Pope*.[83] The review of the second volume, however, is only an account and paraphrase of Warton's work, mostly made of direct quotations, with occasional appreciations, such as "interesting," "uncommon," "entertaining," "amusing," "enriched," "enlivened." A reference to Volume II as "just published" occurs also in the June, 1782, number of the *Gentleman's Magazine*.[84] As a matter of fact, it had been published before February of that year, since it was reviewed in the *Critical Review* of that month.

In 1778, the *Essay* was violently attacked by Percival

[80] LII, 236-40.
[81] *Ibid.*, p. 236.
[81a] LII, 239 f.
[82] LIII, 97-108.
[83] XXVII (1769), 280-89.
[84] LII, 289.

Stockdale in *An Enquiry into the Nature and Genuine Laws of Poetry.*

WARTON'S EDITION OF POPE'S WORKS

Warton's edition of Pope would not concern us here except for its close relation to the *Essay* and the criticism that Warton received for using so much of the *Essay* in making the notes for the edition of Pope. It seems well, therefore, to give a short account of this, Warton's last and largest labor. As to the task of properly annotating—hunting up obscure references and not depending on biographical dictionaries and professional helps but rather reading widely in older as well as in contemporary literature—see some bright sentences in Mark Pattison's review of Elwin's edition of Pope.[85] Pattison thinks that Warton's notes were brought together from a desire to replace Warburton's argumentative commentary, and in accordance with what Warton believed to be a just and appropriate method of annotating a classic.[86]

Warton writes on February 6, 1792, to his friend John Wilkes, who, at a dinner in his house had publicly proposed that Warton and he should make a new, complete edition of Pope, that he is flattered and that the prospect is "pleasant and profitable." He adds that he will not lose sight of it, and that he should be happy to have Wilkes as a fellow-laborer. Then he asks about the relations of a new editor to the present proprietors of the copy, saying that probably the "right, by this time, must be extinguished."[87] After the completion of the

---

[85] *British Quarterly Review,* LV (1872), 413-46. Reprinted as "Pope and His Editors," in Pattison's *Essays,* II, 350-95.

[86] In a letter to Hayley, December 29, 1795, Warton says, "I have been forced to give *hard blows* to the marvellous absurdities of Warburton."—Wooll, *Memoirs,* p. 405.

[87] John Wilkes, "Select Correspondence," XI (1754-1797), British Museum, Add. MSS. 30877, fol. 116.

edition,[88] Warton writes Wilkes from Wickham, July 17, 1797, saying, "It would be a gross affectation in me to deny that I am made very happy indeed by your friendly approval of my Pope, a work which it will be very easy for every common reader to carp at and censure, whose cavils I am prepared to expect and despise."[89] He adds that one approval by Wilkes outweighs a thousand such attacks.

Regarding a review of his work, Warton writes to Wilkes from Wickham, September 30, 1797: "Do you see, or is it worth your while to see, how I have been attacked in the last *Monthly Review*. Principally because I, a grave Doctor, should have dared to insert in my edition of Pope the 'Sober Advice from Horace,' and the admirable Pleading of Scriblerus concerning 'The Double Mistress,' both which Pope himself had inserted in an Edition published by his friend Dodsley. I cannot but smile at such an impotent attack. *Nisi moveat cimex Pantilius.* . . . The same good critic is also angry that I should have interwoven what I had before said in my 'Essay on Pope': —to do which, was one of the principal motives for my undertaking the edition. You may be assured I laid my account and expected to be attacked, and therefore bear such a bombardment with patience and insensibility."[90]

The same reviewer of whom Warton speaks above points out that Pope is of the class of poets whose text needs illustrations and elucidations because of his treatment of local and temporary topics, with allusions to persons and events. Warburton's edition is censured because the Bishop expatiated on

---

[88] December 29, 1795, he writes Hayley that he has finished his labors on Pope for the Press and "We have begun to print." Wooll, *Memoirs*, p. 405.

[89] Cf. Wilkes, "Select Correspondence," as above, fol. 139.

[90] *Ibid.*, fol. 143. See also Nichols, *Literary Anecdotes*, IX (1815), 475; and the *Monthly Review*, XXIII (Second Series, August, 1797), 361-71. Cf. also Edith J. Morley, "Joseph Warton: a Comparison of His *Essay on the Genius and Writings of Pope* with His Edition of Pope's *Works*," in *Essays and Studies by Members of the English Association*, IX (1924), 98 ff.

AN ESSAY ON THE GENIUS AND WRITINGS OF POPE.

The THIRD EDITION, Corrected.

Satyra quidem tota noſtra eſt: in qua primus inſignem laudem adeptus eſt Lucilius; qui quoſdam ita deditos ſibi adhuc habet amatores, ut eum, non ejuſdem modo operis autoribus, ſed omnibus poetis, præferre non dubitent.

QUINTILIAN.

LONDON,
PRINTED FOR J. DODSLEY, IN PALL-MALL.
MDCCLXXII.

Title-page of the legitimate third edition of Joseph Warton's "An Essay on . . . Pope," 1772.

the subject-matter of Pope's works, mistaking his meaning and paying off his own enemies or opponents. Notes of the type of Warton's, he adds, are needed, being exact illustrations of Pope's meaning and allusions.

But he claims that Warton had appropriated most of the unexceptionable of Warburton's notes and had merely digested, under the appropriate pages, the greater part of his own *Essay on Pope, totidem verbis.* He adds that Warton gives a few notes from other editors, but only from well known books, and that there is "*some* original matter."

Warton's summary of the literary character of Pope is given in full by this reviewer, with only a few qualifications suggested. He then selects a few of the items that strike him as new or worthy of remark, matters that throw light on Pope rather than Warton. His summary of the edition is excellent. He says that it is an improvement over Warburton, that it is rather careless work, that it is too much a transcript of the editor's previous work, especially as this was less mature in taste and judgment and not "always in harmony with later opinions," that even Warton's transcription of his own words is careless and repetitious, that more should have been done in tracing Pope's imitations and resemblances to other poets, and that the whole seems hastily done. Wooll declares the "plagiarism (if the stealing from himself merits the title) inevitable" and "unavoidable."[91]

Concerning this review, Warton wrote to John Nichols, September 13, 1797, "I have a little inclination to know, and perhaps you may be able to inform me, who is the writer of a peevish, feeble, and therefore contemptible criticism, on the edition of Pope, published in the last *Monthly Review*. The good man seems to be principally angry at my inserting the observations formerly made in my *Essay* on Pope, which it

[91] P. 81.

ORIGIN, SIGNIFICANCE, RECEPTION 33

would have been absurd, and improper, and impossible, and contrary to the very design of undertaking the Edition, not to have done; and if they had been omitted, then I should have been called on for such an unexpected omission. I am too callous a veteran to regard such sort of objections, etc."[92] He says the same thing on September 30, 1797, to John Wilkes.[93]

Concerning this edition, George Steevens wrote to Bishop Percy, September 9, 1797, after referring to this review, "I wish our venerable friend had not undertaken this work at so late a period of his life. But though it will add little to his reputation, for his trouble he received no less a sum than five hundred pounds."[94]

One other review of this edition is mentioned by Warton in his letter to Wilkes on September 30, 1797. He says, "But I have been only this morning informed, that I have been unmercifully scourged in the *last* Edition of 'The Pursuits of Literature,'[95] which I have not seen. I much wish you could hear, and would let me know, who is the Author of that strange work. Surely the verse part of it is the most harsh, crabbed, and obscure, that has been produced since the days of Persius, and evidently written for the sake of long pedantic notes. One shall hardly see such Drawcansir-work. Every body is censured and abused. The Satirist defies discovery, saying it will be impossible to find him out. Yet I am of the opinion we shall at last drag out into the light of day this literary *cacus* . . . *incendia vana vomentem.* . . . All I say relates to the *first* edition, not having seen the last. Give me a line on the subject."[96]

[92] Nichols, *Literary Anecdotes*, VI, 174 n.
[93] See above, p. 30.   [94] Nichols, *op. cit.*, VII, 30.
[95] By T. J. Mathias (1754?-1835), English satirist and Italian scholar.
[96] Wilkes, *op. cit.*, fol. 143. See also Nichols, *op. cit.*, IX (1815), 475.

II

A HISTORY OF THE FIVE EDITIONS

THE VALUE OF SUCH A STUDY

COMMENTING on an addition made by Pope to the first edition of the *Essay on Man,* Warton says that "it is a pleasing amusement to trace out the alterations that a great writer gradually makes in his own works."[1] In addition to the "amusement" that comes from watching the growth of judgment and taste of a writer, the study of the history of Warton's *Essay* during his lifetime is profitable for several reasons. In the first place, it exhibits the general change in critical consciousness from "classical" to "romantic" canons in the middle of the eighteenth century. Secondly, such a study is profitable very particularly as reflecting this change in the matter of contemporary literary reputations. That his contemporaries felt this is shown by an anonymous reviewer of Warton's second volume, who says, "so closely are [sic] *the Genius and Writings of Pope* necessarily connected with most of the literary characters of his time, as well as of former ages, that many of them also pass in review before us, and contribute largely to the entertainment and information of the reader."[2] The successive editions of the *Essay* note the publication of new works and show the changes in critical principles due to them. They show Warton rapidly becoming aware of the value of his critical principles, strengthening them, and applying them more specifically. He helped establish anew the facts that both the critical and the creative work of a period show the same general tendencies, that good work is praised, though often hes-

[1] *Essay on Pope,* II (4th ed.), 78.
[2] *Gentleman's Magazine,* LII (May, 1782), 240.

HISTORY OF THE FIVE EDITIONS   35

itatingly, by contemporaries, and that the domination of Pope was sharply questioned both in poetry and in criticism within ten years after his death.

The analysis of Warton's successive editions shows, thirdly, how rapidly and in what details the work of Gray, Collins, Mason, and other "romantic" poets was winning its way, creating new standards of literary judgment, and modifying the absolute standards of the late seventeenth and early eighteenth centuries. And finally it shows, though not so clearly as the contemporary work of Thomas Warton, Jr., the appearance at this time of the new historical and relative criticism which soon became central in romantic theory.[3] Warton remained, in most things, all his life under the dominion of Aristotelian absolute standards, but in the few matters here shown, he feels and acts upon the principle of judging writing with reference to the historical circumstances under which it was produced.[4]

THE FIRST EDITION, 1756

Soon after finishing his Virgil in 1753, Warton began preparing his *Essay*. That he was at work on it is shown in a letter to his brother of May 16, 1754, saying, "I greatly fear I shall not have much copy by the 6th of June"—and gives the reasons why.[5] He visited Spence at Byfleet in the summer of 1754 and undoubtedly took much from Spence's *Essay on Pope's Translation of the Odyssey* and put it directly into his new work. On May 20, 1755, he writes to his brother, "I am not idle with respect to Pope."[6] November 9, 1755, Edward Young, to whom Warton proposed to dedicate his *Essay*, wrote, "You do me an honour. I shall not fail to keep your secret" (as to the authorship).[7]

[3] Vol. I (1st and 4th ed.), 132-33, as to judging Cervantes. Cf. above, pp. 6-7.

[4] See the *Essay*, I (1st ed.), 5, 132 f., where he comments on Pope's *Essay on Criticism*, ll. 119-21.   [5] Wooll, *Memoirs*, p. 223.

[6] *Ibid.*, p. 234.   [7] *Ibid.*, p. 236.

In the March, 1756, number of the *Gentleman's Magazine* the *Essay* is announced as published: "An essay on the writings and genius of Mr. Pope. 3s [*sic*] *Cooper*."[8] It was reviewed in the same magazine in the May and June numbers.[9] The first words we have concerning the actual publication of the book are from Robert Dodsley to Warton, April 8, 1756. He says, "Your Essay is publish'd, the price 5s. bound. I gave Mrs. Cooper[10] directions about advertising, and have sent to her this afternoon, to desire she will look after its being inserted in the evening papers. I have a pleasure in telling you that it is lik'd in general, and particularly by such as you would wish should like it. But you have surely not kept your secret: Johnson mention'd it to Mr. Hitch as yours—Dr. Birch mention'd it to Garrick as yours—And Dr. Akenside mention'd it as yours to me—And many more whom I cannot now think on have ask'd for it as yours and your brother's. I have sold many of them in my own shop, and have dispers'd and push'd it as much as I can; and have said more than I could have said if my name had been to it."[11] It was probably for this reason that Straus overlooked the first edition in his fine biography of Dodsley, where he claims to print all the books with whose publication Dodsley had anything to do, whether his name appeared upon the title-page or not.[12] (A facsimile reproduction of this title-page appears above in the frontispiece.)

On April 15, 1756, Johnson wrote Warton, "I have lately seen an octavo book which I suspect to be yours, though I have not yet read above ten pages. That way of publishing without acquainting your friends is a wicked trick."[13] Johnson re-

[8] XXVI, 143.
[9] XXVI, 249-51, 305 f. See above, p. 27.
[10] Concerning Mrs. Cooper as publisher, see above, pp. 12-13.
[11] Wooll, p. 237.
[12] *Op. cit.*, pp. 316 ff.   [13] Wooll, p. 238.

HISTORY OF THE FIVE EDITIONS 37

viewed the volume in the April-May number of the *Literary Magazine*.[14] Garrick wrote Warton on June 15, 1756, saying that he did not know the author of the *Essay* and asking him, if he knew who wrote the book, to give him his thanks for the fine compliment paid to him.[15]

The volume ends with "End of the first Volume." This shows that in 1756 Warton distinctly expected to publish a second volume, a fact established elsewhere in this study by statements of friends and reviewers.[16]

THE SECOND EDITION, 1762

Concerning the value of second and corrected editions, we have the word of Robert Dodsley himself. Writing to Shenstone January 20, 1759, concerning some protest the latter had made against the conventional "Second Editions with Additions and Alterations," Dodsley says, "I shall dispatch this point in a very few words. Would you have an author after he has once published ty'd up from correcting his errors or improving his work? Second thoughts, you know, are said to be best and therefore second editions corrected are no bad thing. I speak as a bookseller."[17]

The second edition of Warton's *Essay* appeared in 1762. One issue, called "The Second Edition, Corrected and Enlarged," was put out in the spring over Mrs. Cooper's name, though she died August 5, 1761,[18] and later in the year another by R. and J. Dodsley themselves. This is called only "The Second Edition Corrected." The only difference between the two is in the rearrangement of the title-page, which

---

[14] See above, p. 25.
[15] Wooll, p. 240; for the compliment to Garrick see the *Essay*, I, 119.
[16] See above, pp. 19-22.
[17] Correspondence between Dodsley and William Shenstone, British Museum, ADD. MSS. 28959, fol. 246.
[18] Nichols, *Literary Anecdotes*, VIII (1814), 403.

was reset by Dodsley, omitting the "and Enlarged" of the former issue and adding the date. I judge that Dodsley thought the word "enlarged" too ambitious for Warton's changes. Warton's name, strangely, does not appear on either issue. Facsimile reproductions of these title-pages may be found on pages 9 and 17 above.

It is possible that Warton proceeded rapidly with Volume II after 1756 (we know he was working at it in 1759), and that this Cooper issue of Volume I was intended to be the first of the two volumes planned. But the printer finished only 200 pages of Volume II and then the work stopped for twenty years. The matter is of slight importance except as showing that he thought highly of his work, was pleased with its reception, and wished to reflect contemporary happenings in the field of letters.

The "corrections" for this second edition are many and substantial, and there are only a few changes which are not continued in the third and fourth—none of critical importance. There are some 247 changes that materially affect the sense. In addition, there are many changes in punctuation and in rhetorical rectification. Warton revised sharply for all the re-issues, but the most interesting and important changes are those for this edition. They are analyzed later.

The title-page is changed from AN/ ESSAY/ ON THE / WRITINGS / AND / GENIUS / OF / POPE. / to AN / ESSAY / ON THE / GENIUS / AND / WRITINGS / OF / POPE. / —at least more logical and more euphonious.

THE PIRATED DUBLIN EDITION, 1764

A pirated edition was published by Peter Wilson, Dame Street, Dublin, and called "The Third Edition, Corrected and

AN ESSAY ON THE GENIUS AND WRITINGS OF POPE.

VOLUME THE SECOND.

LONDON:
PRINTED FOR J. DODSLEY, IN PALL-MALL

M.DCC.LXXXII.

Title-page of the first issue of Volume II of Joseph Warton's "An Essay on . . . Pope," 1782. Later in the same year this volume was reset as part of the complete fourth edition.

Enlarged."[19] I find no mention by Warton of this edition. The title-page is reproduced on page 23 above.

THE THIRD EDITION, 1772

The legitimate third edition appeared in 1772, over the name of J. Dodsley, his brother Robert having died in 1764. This edition is a very handsome volume, with larger pages and uncut edges. There are nine more pages than in the 1762 edition, and the matter is readjusted from page to page. This is due to the fact that Warton made many corrections for this issue, which on the title-page (see page 31 above) is called "corrected." These corrections are traced below among the changes made from edition to edition.

THE FOURTH EDITION AND THE SECOND VOLUME

The second volume was completed and published early in 1782.[20] In the first issue the title-page (see page 39) reads: AN / ESSAY / ON THE / GENIUS / AND / WRITINGS / OF / POPE. /, but the running heads throughout read ESSAY ON THE WRITINGS AND GENIUS OF POPE. Thomas Tyers says in the same year, "Some weeks ago, the second volume of Dr. Warton's made it's appearance."[21] In his Advertisement Warton says that two hundred pages of the volume had been printed "above twenty years ago." Dodsley, then, had kept these two hundred pages in sheets and finished the volume in the same format. The signatures are continuous, with gatherings of four leaves, whereas in the later reprint the gatherings were eight leaves; both are in octavo.

[19] See section on piracies, above, pp. 14-15. This is an exact reprinting of the first edition of 1756.

[20] Professor Philip Parker, of St. John's College, Oxford, notes that there are different issues of this volume, and the one that he describes differs from mine. See his "Notes on the Bibliography of Joseph Warton" intended for the *Bodleian Quarterly Review*.

[21] *An Historical Rhapsody on Mr. Pope* (2d ed., London, 1782), Advertisement, p. x; quoted in Nichols, *Literary Anecdotes*, VIII (1814), 96 n.

HISTORY OF THE FIVE EDITIONS 41

Later in the year Dodsley decided to put out the work in two volumes of uniform size. For this the book was entirely reset, with a slight redistribution of matter on the page, with rearrangement of notes and much change and enlargement in the already printed portion, and section seven was shifted from volume two to volume one to equalize the size of the volumes. The pages of the new volumes had a somewhat larger and wider end and a slightly larger page of print. Altogether this edition was a very handsome piece of book making. Facsimile reproductions of the title-pages of the two volumes may be found on pages 51 and 55 below.

For this full fourth edition Warton revised extensively, while retaining all the important revisions that he had made for the second and third editions. Yet I find no difference in style between the portions previously printed and the remainder. In the second issue (in two volumes), late in the year, the number of corrections in the part printed twenty years earlier, as compared with the number of corrections in the remainder, is in the proportion of approximately 54 to 46 per cent. In pages 1-200 there are 125 alterations and enlargements; in pages 201-481 there are 106, making a total of 231. One would think that in reprinting matter written so long before, the critic would have corrected even more freely. The fact that he did not do so may suggest that the whole was in manuscript early in 1762 and that the second half was sent to the printer without rewriting. It is strange that these printed sheets were allowed to lie uncompleted in Dodsley's shop for two decades, while Warton lived only a few hours' ride from London and must often have been in town and seen his publisher.[22]

Thus, twenty-six years after the first appearance, the book was completed, had been recently revised throughout, and

[22] As to his delay, see above, pp. 19-22.

represented Warton's mature judgment, though, as seen before, he seems to have intended to issue another edition in 1792.[23]

THE FIFTH EDITION, 1806

Finally, six years after Warton's death, and fifty years after the first appearance of the *Essay*, the last edition was printed.[24] I judge that this was issued in connection with, or to take advantage of, the publicity resulting from the appearance of Wooll's *Biographical Memoirs* of Warton, which appeared in the same year. For the first time Warton's name appears on the title-page. This edition is a close reprint of the fourth, though there are some unimportant corrections, chiefly changes in references to Pope's lines and to books cited. The text was reset, of course, and the matter from page to page differs a little, though the total number of pages is about the same. But the punctuation is greatly modernized—twenty-four years had passed since the printing of the fourth edition, and, with them, eighteenth-century styles of printing. Evidently the edition was carefully supervised. An Index was added. The book was printed by Thomas Maiden for W. J. and J. Richardson and fourteen others. Notes and changes made by Warton for his own intended fifth edition[25] are not extant or are yet to be discovered. Facsimile reproductions of the title-pages of this edition may be found on pages 63 and 67 below.

[23] See above, p. 24.

[24] H. W. Garrod in his *Wordsworth: Lectures and Essays* (Oxford, 1st ed. 1923, and again 2d ed. 1927, p. 155) made the mistake of saying that a new edition of the *Essay* appeared in 1798 and was noticed in the *Monthly Magazine* for July of that year. There is no mention of Warton in this number. In the August number Warton's edition of Pope (1797) is the subject of a letter to the editor (VI, 88).

[25] See above, p. 24.

III

SUMMARY OF THE CHANGES MADE IN THE FIVE EDITIONS

IT is noticeable that from edition to edition the changes fall into rather well-defined classes. They divide naturally into two chief groups. One group consists of those due to bookishness, the desire to make a "correct" and readable book. Such are corrections of mere errors, omissions of irrelevant matter, closer citations and references, the giving of sources and additional matter. The other group consists of those due to growth of information and taste and to Warton's taking notice of recent events in the realm of letters.

A numerical summary of all the changes gives the following result:

From the 1st to the 2nd edition, vol. I	247
From the 2nd to the 3rd edition, vol. I	69
From the 3rd to the 4th edition, vol. I	82
From the 1st to the 4th edition, vol. II	212
Total	610

TECHNICAL AND BOOKISH CHANGES

Among the modifications due to Warton's desire to make his book more workmanlike, the following types are distinguished:[1]

---

[1] The first three types cover so many and such unimportant changes as not to merit citation; so references to examples are deliberately omitted.

It would be useless and nearly impossible to refer to all the changes in the successive editions of the *Essay*. I have used only the most interesting or significant though I have classified and summarized all. Since the first four editions are rare, my page references are to the more accessible fifth edition (1806). But when I am dealing with a specific edition, I give exact references to that. Readers can easily find passages in the fifth edition by noticing that Warton regularly numbers the passages from Pope which he is referring to and that his section headings give the poems he is treating.

(a) Corrections of mere errors, such as false spelling, misprints, wrong punctuation, omissions of words in quotations, misuse of words, wrong references, mistakes in grammar, and improper inclusion of citation in the text instead of among the footnotes. Under this head would come a few words which were changing their spelling, as *landschape* to *landscape* (this word varies indifferently between the two forms from edition to edition), and the substitution of current for obsolescent forms of expression, as "answered" for "answered to." In one case the change makes a grammatical error, *is* (1st and 2nd editions) to *are* (3rd and 4th).[2] Of the class of changes the 2nd edition gives us 46, the 3rd, 5, and the 4th, 5. Similar changes in the second volume are 11, a total of 67 changes for 838 pages of print.

(b) Another body of unimportant changes consists of retranslation of quotations from French and the classics. There are 55 of these in the 2nd edition, none afterward. Some make slight changes of meaning; for example, see pages 72, 74, and 75 f., in the 1st edition and pages 70, 72, and 73 f. respectively in the second.

(c) We have some 18 changes in spelling of names, personal titles and care about dates and titles of books. A few are evidently for the sake of consistency, but most are unsystematic or merely haphazard. Ben Johnson often becomes Jonson, as was taking place everywhere in the middle of the century to distinguish him from Dr. Samuel. Yet Warton has some instances of the older spelling in his last revision. So it is with regard to Spenser; usually it is so, but early and late we find Spencer, always when quoting from Pope, who uses that spelling. It is Boccace or Boccacio without any order, Fontaine and La Fontaine, Bruyere and La Bruyere. He corrects Mr. to Dr. Lowth, omits Mr. before Dryden's name.

[2] Cf. II (4th ed.), 353 n., and 385.

CHANGES MADE IN THE FIVE EDITIONS 45

He changes the title of Francis Peck's book from *Miscellanea Curiosa* to *Memoirs of the Life and Writings of Milton* (which is still inexact) and adds the citation of DeClugny's epitaph on Abelard. The first edition (1756) is so dated on the title-page; in the second edition (1762) the Cooper issue has no date, the Dodsley issue later in the year has it on the title-page; in the third edition (1772) the date is both on the title-page and at the end of the Dedication to Dr. Young.

(d) Three changes are of errors of some importance: in the first three editions he said that Crebillon imitated the *Orestes* of Sophocles, this he corrects in the fourth to the *Electra*;[3] he first said that the French "at present" produce little besides Novels and Memoirs, but in his last revision he omits this absurd statement;[4] in 1756 he says he was of this same critical opinion "at first" but justifies the lines of Pope which he is discussing, because he has been "informed" that they are an allusion to Pope's own experience with an unfortunate lady, "for whom he had conceived a violent passion."[5]

(e) A few changes omit citations and references to authorities. In 1756 when speaking of the argument that "a seeming originality" does not necessarily indicate barrenness of invention, he added as "a late critic has urged." The reference to the critic is continued till 1782, and then omitted as out of date or as poor taste in thus giving the support of authority to a commonly accepted opinion.[6] He omits in the second edition his own name from a quotation from his poem *Isis*.[7] At first, concerning Ariosto, he said that "the best and most judicious account I know of the genius of Ariosto" was contained in his brother Thomas Warton's *Observations on the Faerie Queene of Spenser*. He removes this in 1762, giving

[3] I (3rd ed.), 271; (4th ed.), 273. [4] I (3rd ed.), 156; (4th ed.), 155.
[5] I (1st ed.), 133; (2nd ed.), 333 f.
[6] I (3rd ed.), 89; (4th ed.), 90.
[7] I (1st ed.), 213 n.; (2nd ed.), 210 n.

instead a quotation from Hume's *Four Dissertations*, which had appeared in 1757.[8] He quotes from Baretti's "just translation" of Dante and cites his *Dissertation*. The citations disappear in 1772, to give place to an irrelevant compliment to Sir Joshua Reynolds.[9] In 1782 he omits a second statement that a common belief about Horace's *Epistle to the Pisones* "has been lately confuted" (by Hurd in his paper on the epistle), because he had already made the point.[10] In the first edition of Volume Two he cites Martinelli's "defense" of Ariosto in his *Letters Familiari e criticke*, published in 1758. In the revision of the same year he omits it entirely.[11] From the same volume is omitted a reference to Walpole's *Anecdotes of Painting in England* illustrating Milton's vigorous imagination.[12] A special reference to Bishop Hoadly's published contempt for Berkeley's *Alciphron* is omitted from the fourth edition, Volume Two, and the same statement is merely made vaguely of "writers."[13]

(f) We have some eighteen instances of translating quotations from Latin and French authors (which had before appeared without the English), probably to increase the popularity of the book. The Advertisement to the third edition (1772) says, "Whenever a quotation is made in the French language, throughout the following remarks, the author desires to be understood, that he is far from thinking the use of that language any particular decoration to his style; he only uses French words, when the force and meaning of the passages so quoted depend on the peculiar turn and idiom of the original." Evidently he had been criticized for this tendency toward

---

[8] I (1st ed.), 243 n.; (2nd ed.), 240 n.
[9] I (2nd ed.), 253 n.; (3rd ed.), 262 n.
[10] I (3rd ed.), 172; (4th ed.), 171.
[11] II (1st ed.), 97 n.; (4th ed.), 34 n.
[12] II (1st ed.), 241 n.; (4th ed.), 183 n.
[13] (1st ed.), 264 n.; (4th ed.), 204 n.

affectation and thought to correct it. Ten of the translations are from French, six from Latin, and two from Greek. In one instance the Latin text and the English translation are both given, and another is a free paraphrase only. All the quotations translated are from literary criticism and illustrations, and not from texts of literary masterpieces. Of these latter there are hundreds of untranslated passages.

(g) In twenty-one cases Warton silently omits words, phrases, and sentences because they seem needless, the remaining matter being adequate to his thought. Sometimes the omitted matter is irrelevant or merely in poor taste, and in a few instances illustrative citations from the classics are not very close. These omissions are about evenly divided among the successive revisions,—7 in the first, 4 in the second, and 5 in the third and 5 in the second volume from its first to its later issue.

(h) In a few interesting instances Warton, when he revises, gives the source of an idea or fact, or gives a striking parallel statement. He perhaps fears he may be charged with plagiarism, or he has a conscientious desire to give the proper credit, or he has discovered the parallelism after his previous publication. Two instances are typical. His fundamental thesis is that there is an essential difference between a man of wit and a true poet. In a paragraph of the Dedication dealing with this subject he adds in the second edition the sentence, "It is remarkable, that Dryden says of Donne, 'He was the greatest wit, though not the greatest poet, of this nation.' "[14] In the Dedication to *Eleanora*, from which this is taken, Dryden calls his poem a "panegyrical poem." So in this same edition in the new classified list of poets in the Dedication Warton adds the term "panegyrical" to the previous terms "moral and ethical" describing the class in which Dryden is placed.[15]

[14] I, iv. Cf. Dryden, *Works*, ed. cit., XI, 123.
[15] I (2nd ed.), xi.

On the occasion of Warton's many visits to Spence in 1754 and later, his friend gave him many anecdotes of Pope.[16] In Warton's first volume he did not give Spence as his authority; but in the second volume (1782) after the 201 pages printed before 1762, he did add his authority, placing it sometimes in footnotes, oftener in the text,[17] and in the full revision later in the year, he quotes Spence many times as the source of his information.

(i) A large number of corrections, some 60 in all, are improvements in style—for coherence, for more exact presentation of cited matter, for the avoidance of repetition and unharmonious collocations of sounds, from a desire to secure variety, in order to avoid pedantry, or to obtain exact reference within sentences. We have several examples of breaking up previous statements into new sentences, and even into paragraphs, for better emphasis and to please the eye. Evidently Warton cared for his book and rather lovingly corrected its defects.

(j) A group of changes consists of modifications to avoid anachronisms. In the first edition (1756) we have many dates and many specifications of matters "lately," "of late," "at present." These became increasingly out of date, six, sixteen, and twenty-six years after. In 1756, '62, and '72 Warton was willing to say, "I am sensible . . . of what a late critic has urged that. . . ." But in 1782 he changes it to "I well know that. . . ." This would show that Warton was scrupulous in giving credit, though the opinion referred to might be commonplace enough. As before mentioned, he thinks it needful to inform the reader that the anachronisms of the first two hundred pages are due to the fact that they were printed over twenty years before. Yet, in spite of this apology and of the correction of many such contradictions, a large number of

---

[16] Vol. I (4th ed.), 80, 389; Vol. II, 20 n., 38 n., 39 n., 55.
[17] Vol. II (4th ed.), 155, 176, 178, 239, 248.

CHANGES MADE IN THE FIVE EDITIONS 49

these "lately"s were left: Harris published his "Discourse on Music, Painting, and Poetry" in his *Three Treatises* in 1744. To refer to this in 1756 as something "lately seen"[18] is not so bad. But to leave it so in 1782 is due either to carelessness or to some deliberate wish to leave the marks of the original occasion upon his work. The reviewer of Warton's edition of Pope's works in the *Monthly Review* for August, 1797,[19] points out this same carelessness and says that Warton merely lifted his illustrative matter from the *Essay*, leaving these anachronisms glaring.

(*k*) Along with these alterations due to a desire to improve the style of expression, comes a small group of changes due to a growing care for closer, more logical thinking. At first (1756) he said that *pity* (arising from reading Isaiah's account of the fall of Babylon) is a stronger sensation than *complacency* (arising from reading Pope's remaking of Isaiah into an eclogue of pleasing images). In 1762 he changes these terms to *terror* and *joy*.[20] "Personifications" is a better term than "personages" in speaking of the art of a dramatist in creating character.[21] At first writers were condemned for ambitiously endeavoring "to be original and new," and so becoming "distorted and unnatural." Later it is "to shine and surprise" and so to become "stiff, and forced, and affected."[22]

Then we have a good deal of hedging, guarding of overstrong statements, apologizing and disclaiming, and insertion of exceptions. He fears he may be judged pretentious if he is thought to be offering a "complete" catalogue of English poets, when he only means to suggest a number of species.[23] To the rule that poets and painters are at their best when about thirty

[18] I (1st ed.), 177 f. Cf. 4th ed., p. 179.
[19] See above, pp. 30-33.
[20] I (1st and 2nd edd.), 14.   [21] I (1st and 2nd edd.), 18.
[22] I (2nd ed.), 201; (3rd ed.), 209.
[23] I (1st and 2nd edd.), xii.

years old,[24] in the next edition we have an exception in favor of Congreve.[25] From 1756 to 1772 Tasso was "the second of the Italian poets"; in 1782 he is "the second or third."[26] In the revision of volume two Boileau's reputation is qualified by the statement that though as a poet his testimony is to be regarded, as "an antiquarian" it is not.[27] Sometimes he modifies to avoid being specific and responsible. In the first three editions he distinctly specified the faults of French tragedies as due to their "declamations"; his last revision ventures only so far as to say that "some of their [the French] most perfect tragedies, abound in faults" contrary to the nature of tragedy.[28] As he revises, his good sense leads him to specify and limit his meanings. To make sure that he is understood, he italicizes words in a passage he is studying.[29] To make sure that we realize the weight of his general assertion as to the faults of French tragedy, he adds in 1772, "even the best of Racine."[30] To make more specific the reasons why Pope is best as a didactic, moral, and satiric poet, he adds a specification in the revision of Volume Two, that "he stuck to describing *modern manners*," and that these are unfit for lofty poetry.[31]

(*l*) The largest number of minor changes consists of the additions of further examples and instances, chiefly from the ancient classics. There are some 124 items in this list: 20 in the second, 16 in the third, and 20 in the fourth edition of Volume One; and 68 in the second edition of Volume Two. It is a very learned book, no less than 550 authors from ancient and modern times being referred to or quoted. Warton seems to have kept the book by him and entered into it illustrations from his wide reading. The list of minor Greek and Latin

[24] I (1st ed.), p. 104.
[25] I (2nd ed.), 101.
[26] I (3rd ed.), 78; (4th ed.), 79.
[30] I (2nd ed.), 199; (3rd ed.), 207.
[31] II (1st ed.), 478; (2nd ed.), 408.
[27] I, 356.
[28] I (3rd ed.), 207; (4th ed.), 208.
[29] I (1st and 2nd edd.), 27.

AN ESSAY ON THE GENIUS AND WRITINGS OF POPE.

IN TWO VOLUMES.

VOL. I.

The FOURTH EDITION, Corrected.

Satyra quidem tota noſtra eſt: in qua primus inſignem laudem adeptus eſt Lucilius; qui quoſdam ita deditos ſibi adhuc habet amatores, ut eum, non ejuſdem modo operis autoribus, ſed omnibus poetis, præferre non dubitent.

QUINTILIAN.

LONDON:
PRINTED FOR J. DODSLEY, IN PALL-MALL.
M.DCC.LXXXII.

Title-page of the fourth edition of Volume I of Joseph Warton's "An Essay on . . . Pope," 1782.

critics is noticeably large; that of French critics from the middle of the seventeenth century on is at least liberal. He was regarded as a learned, even heavily learned, man by his contemporaries, and I find no contemporary impeachment of either the breadth or trustworthiness of his scholarship except by the reviewer of his edition of Pope.[32] In recent criticism most of this "learning" is considered irrelevant or merely pedantic, but not inaccurate or showy. The second volume is more frequently illustrated than the first, partly because his examples have been longer accumulating and partly because it deals with the portion of Pope's work which closely imitates classical literature and therefore invites comparison and the tracing of influences. One or two instances will illustrate the kind of addition here listed. In the second edition of Volume One, page 297, he adds a paragraph in the text to give a list of poetical epistles of the Italian, Leonardo Bruni.[33] He is illustrating Pope's *Epistle of Eloisa to Abelard* and has referred to Ovid, Propertius, Fenton, Drayton, and Hervey. An almost accidental fling at Chapelain's style in quoting from Boileau's *Satires* leads Warton to add a defense of Chapelain, with a reference to d'Olivet's *History* of the French Academy (1729).[34] The second volume of Gibbon's *History* appeared in 1781. Warton mentions it (1782) in connection with his judgment of the excellence of the style of Tacitus.[35]

CHANGES DUE TO GROWTH IN TASTE AND JUDGMENT

The second general class of changes in the successive editions consists of those due to growth of taste, of information, and of critical judgment. The first edition was the work of

[32] See above, p. 32.
[33] Bruni (Leonardo) *Aretino* (miscalled "Antonio" by Warton), *Epistolæ familiares*. Cf. *Essay*, I (1st ed.), 298.
[34] II (1st ed.), 284 f.; (4th ed.), 223.
[35] II (1st ed.), 227; (4th ed.), 169.

CHANGES MADE IN THE FIVE EDITIONS 53

a man of only thirty-three, too young to have the ripeness required for permanent critical work. The successive revisions show that he grew rapidly; they show also that he took full cognizance of contemporary happenings in the literary world—a matter of great importance in tracing the growth of eighteenth-century criticism.

(a) Such a growth of taste is seen in his change of personal to impersonal statement, and in dropping references to himself and his brother Thomas. Of this we have ten instances, most of them in the second edition (1762). He drops several references to poems he has "lately" seen, about which he expresses various judgments.[36] He at first had references to his own and his brother's poems, though often they are not cited under their own names. Such poor taste was well corrected.[37] From the phrase "our Shakespear" he drops the sentimental pronoun.[38] Only once does he add a personal note to a later edition—when, speaking of a bas-relief by Michelangelo, he adds, "which I have seen."[39] A slight tempest was raised when Warton, in 1756, commenting on line 60 of Pope's *Essay on Criticism*, "One science only will one genius fit," wrote, "some nicer virtuosi here remarked, that in the serious pieces, into which Hogarth has deviated from the natural bias of his genius, there are some strokes of the Ridiculous discernible, which suit not with the dignity of the subject";[40] two instances and one exception are given. This criticism angered Hogarth, who then introduced a publication of Warton's into one of his satiric prints. Chancellor Hoadly in a letter to Warton, April 21, 1757, claimed that Hogarth

[36] E.g. I (1st ed.), 9 f.; (2nd ed.), 9.
[37] E.g. I (1st ed.), 33 f.; (2nd ed.), 33. From I (1st ed.), 213 n. "Warton" is dropped, though the name of the poem, "Isis," is kept; see I (2nd ed.), 210 n.
[38] I (1st ed.), 104; (2nd ed.), 101.
[39] I (3rd ed.), 265 n.; (4th ed.), 267 n.
[40] I (1st e.d), 122.

had never deliberately put malicious bits into his prints, and that Warton was in grave error in saying that he had. Then Warton sent to Hogarth by Hoadly an acknowledgment that he had erred. Hogarth accepted the apology and sent copies of the prints to show Warton's mistake.[41] Yet Garrick wrote to Warton in January, 1762, saying that he had just been with Hogarth and had told him humorously of a dreadful "attack" upon him by Warton. Hogarth was very uneasy, confused— "much hurt." Then Garrick told him the method Warton had actually taken to revenge the injuries he had received in Hogarth's engraving. Garrick was referring to Warton's promise to remove the offending passage, which he fulfilled later in 1762, adding in a footnote a very handsome apology.[42] Hogarth, disconcerted, offered to destroy the plate in which Warton's name is mentioned, for "he would not be overdone in kindness."[43]

(b) A group of alterations showing growth in manly taste are those changing exaggerated, over-exact, and dogmatic statements to those better considered, of which we have twenty-nine examples. Where he was absolute at first, he later qualifies; for example, "it seems that" becomes "it is reported that," "some of" passes into "shall I say," "it appears . . . that" is transformed into "it is possible . . . that,"[44] "almost all" of an inheritance is changed to "a great part."[45] In 1756 and 1762 he said that the satiric épopée is "never used by the ancients"; in 1772 it is "seldom, if ever."[46] Addison's tragedy of *Cato* was at first "heavy and declamatory"; this is lightened to "sententious and declamatory."[47] Dr. Lowth's Latin poem giving

---

[41] The whole incident is related in the Chancellor's letter and in a note in Wooll, p. 246.
[42] I (2nd ed.), 118 f. and n.
[43] Wooll, p. 247 n.
[44] I (1st ed.), 87; (2nd ed.), 84.
[45] I (1st ed.), 108; (2nd ed.), 105.
[46] I (2nd ed.), 202; (3rd ed.), 210.
[47] I (2nd ed.), 258; (3rd ed.), 268.

AN ESSAY

ON THE

GENIUS

AND

WRITINGS

OF

POPE.

IN TWO VOLUMES.

VOL. II.

LONDON:

PRINTED FOR J. DODSLEY, IN PALL-MALL.

M.DCC.LXXXII.

Title-page of the second issue of Volume II as part of the fourth edition of Joseph Warton's "An Essay on . . . Pope," 1782.

Isaiah's description of the Messiah treading the wine-press was in 1756 and 1762 judged "equal to any description in Virgil"; by 1772 it is only "equal to many."[48] Pope's "Ode for Musick on St. Cecilia's Day" was from the first "indisputably the second of the kind," but in 1782 the over-strong adverb is dropped.[49] In this last revision he sees that his exaggerated statement that the French at present produce little besides "Novels and Memoirs" is false and in bad taste; the clause disappears.[50]

At the same time the critic grew more confident in some of his statements and inserted changes making for good taste and for a dignified temperance. At first he was "perhaps ashamed or afraid to speak out in plain English" his opinion of Pope; six years later he is only "unwilling" so to speak."[51] In the first edition of Volume Two, in speaking of Milton's vigorous and creative imagination, Warton had a reference to Walpole's *Anecdotes*. Later in the year this is supplanted by the following enthusiastic encomium: "How astonishing, that his spirit could not be diminished or crushed, by poverty, danger, blindness, disgrace, solitude, and old age!"[52] Warton steadily grew in his enthusiasm for Milton, a sure mark of the changing basis of literary criticism of his age.

(c) It seems well to raise into a separate category a number of changes in which Warton heightens the degree of a statement or widens its application: "What is there very sublime or very Pathetic in POPE?" in 1756 becomes in the second edition "What is there transcendently Sublime or Pathetic in POPE";[53] in the same issue "Voltaire has often been deeply indebted" to Henault, where at first there was no specification

---

[48] I (2nd and 3rd edd.), 19. [49] I (3rd ed.), 51; (4th ed.), 52.
[50] I (3rd ed.), 156; (4th ed.), 155.
[51] I (1st and 2nd edd.), x.
[52] II (1st ed.), p. 241 n.; (4th ed.), p. 183 n.
[53] I (1st and 2nd edd.), x.

CHANGES MADE IN THE FIVE EDITIONS 57

of frequency;[54] "undoubtedly" is added to strengthen a statement, and throughout his revisions, "something" is altered to "somewhat";[55] italics are occasionally employed for the sake of emphasis;[56] Addison's "opera of Rosamond" becomes his "elegant opera of Rosamond,"[57] and Racine's *Athaliah* (i.e. *Athalie*) has its qualification raised from nothing to "admirable Athaliah";[58] till 1782 "Virgil may however have given the hint" for a line of Pope's, but in the last edition doubt disappears entirely;[59] when he revises Volume Two, he adds the clause, "a writer far superior to his son," to the bare mention of "Crebillon the father";[60] in the same volume he first gave the statement that Barford borrowed from Pope the machinery of the sylphs (used in the *Rape of the Lock*) from hearsay, and this is strengthened, when the volume is revised, into an undoubted fact.[61] These two sections have specifications enough to show that Warton constantly and carefully revised his work, modifying over-strong statements in poor or bad taste and growing more confident in his critical judgment. This strengthening of his assertions is especially shown in his judgment of Milton.[62]

(d) These minor modifications lead us to some that are more fundamental, which imply a genuine growth in taste, in critical acumen or range, and in the use of new information to modify preceding points of view. While it must be a flexible and perhaps personal catalog of instances, there are more than thirty examples of this type of change.

Nothing, for instance, is more characteristic of the entire classical movement in criticism than its deliberate pleasure in ranking, placing, classifying of writers, though these classes

---

[54] (1st and 2nd edd.), p. 23 n. [55] I (1st and 2nd edd.), 2.
[56] I (1st ed.), 92 n.; (2nd ed.), 89 n.
[57] I (3rd ed.), 56; (4th ed.), 57. [58] I (3rd ed.), 272 (4th ed.), 274.
[59] I (3rd ed.), 337 n.; (4th ed.), 339 n.
[60] (1st ed.), p. 191; (4th ed.), p. 134.
[61] (1st ed.), p. 284; (4th ed.), p. 222.
[62] See his note on Milton's style, first appearing II (4th ed.), 156.

shift as taste changes. It is the appearance in criticism of Pope's celebrated "ORDER [i.e., ranking] is Heaven's first law."[63] The practice continues far into the Romantic Movement and of course reappears whenever classical, ordering minds are at work, as with Arnold and Saintsbury. In Warton's first volume we have, at the end of his Dedication, his classification of English poets. The errors in judgment here are many and reveal sad limitations in his critical attainments. It will be seen, however, that he shows marked improvement in his revision six years later. The lists are given together, that the changes may be readily seen.

	1st Edition (1756)	*2nd Edition* (1762)	
Class I.	Spenser	Spenser	
	Shakespeare	Shakespeare	
	Milton	Milton	
	"And then, at proper intervals,"		
	Otway		
	Lee		
II.	Dryden	Dryden	Garth
	Donne	Prior	Fenton
	Denham	Addison	Gay
	Cowley	Cowley	Denham
	Congreve	Waller	Parnell
III.	Prior	Butler	
	Waller	Swift	
	Parnell	Rochester	
	Swift	Donne	
	Fenton	Dorset	
		Oldham	

[63] *An Essay on Man*, "Epistle IV," 1. 49.

IV. Pitt   Pitt
    Sandys   Sandys
    Fairfax   Fairfax
    Broome   Broome
    Buckingham   Buckingham
    Lansdowne   Lansdowne

The changes are these: Otway and Lee are dropped, not only from the first class, but entirely from the list—it seems not merely obtuseness, but even perversity, which led to their having been placed in this class; Donne is dropped from the second to the third division; Prior, Waller, Fenton, and Parnell are elevated one degree; Congreve is dropped entirely; Addison, Garth, and Gay are added to the class headed by Dryden; Butler, Rochester, Dorset, and Oldham are given places in the third rank; the first revision drops only the three names referred to. In the last two editions the list remains as in the second.

A similar instance of malinformation and critical astigmatism is found in Warton's list of five ages, "in which the human mind has exerted itself in an extraordinary manner." There is not a name from the spacious days of Queen Elizabeth, though forty-eight are given from the fifty years on the two sides of 1700.[64]

The quicksand of oblivion has made sad havoc with Warton's lists, and the rediscovery of the great Elizabethans by the romantic critics at the beginning of the nineteenth century, or less than forty years after Warton's last revision, has replaced many of them with poets Warton should have known. Doubtless the few names still left in his classification would be kept there by modern students, save that a class must be constituted between Warton's first and second, in which only Dryden of his list is worthy to go.

[64] I, 181 f.

(e) Many small pieces of crude or sentimental criticism disappear before a growing taste. A foolish exaggeration that the stanza on the Magna Charta from the "Ode" in Gilbert West's dramatic poem, *The Institution of the Order of the Garter*, "contains almost all the different measures of which the English language seems capable" silently disappears at the first revision.[65] In the same way does an irrelevant and tasteless rebuke of Bayle, the encyclopædist, for his discussion of the difference in pleasure between concupiscence and genuine affection.[66] From the same motives, a passage is omitted in 1772 containing a long story of the mutilation of Greek prisoners by castration, used at first as illustrative of the experiences of Abelard.[67]

Warton's attitude toward Voltaire shows lively but changing reactions. He is intensely aware of everything Voltaire writes. He is now excessively deferential and now hesitatingly, fearsomely contemptuous. The Frenchman is quoted no less than 14 times (8 in Volume One, 6 in Volume Two), often at length. In most cases Warton disagrees with him. There is, however, some growth in deference, caution, and taste. Up to 1772 Voltaire is "that lively maintainer of many a paradox." In 1782 this is omitted; and a statement immediately following, that a reason he advances is "very strange and inconclusive" is weakened to "not very solid and conclusive."[68] In the first edition of Volume Two Voltaire had "lately advanced" the "outrageous paradox" that the *Orlando* of Ariosto is to be preferred to the *Odyssey* of Homer. To the translation from Voltaire Warton had added this note: "However M. de Voltaire might laugh at the quoting to him a father of the church, yet the following sensible observation on Homer, might be

---

[65] I (1st ed.), 69 f.; (2nd ed.), 67 f.
[66] I (1st ed.), 310 n.; (2nd ed.), 309.
[67] I (2nd ed.), 322-4; (3rd ed.), 334.
[68] I (3rd ed.), 21 f.; (4th ed.), 22.

CHANGES MADE IN THE FIVE EDITIONS 61

worth his consideration"; then followed a few words in Greek from the "Divine" Chrysostom (Orat. 18).[69] The note is omitted from the fourth edition of the *Essay* a few months later, Warton doubtless having learned of his error.[70] In the revision of this volume we have this addition: "Voltaire, it must be owned, writes prose with remarkable elegance, precision, and force."[71] Voltaire published his *Essay on the Epic Poets* in 1728. Warton knew this *Essay* and in his desire to convict Voltaire "not only of outrageous paradox but of inconsistency" seized on a revision of the essay in Voltaire's Complete Works published at Geneva in 1757, Tome XIII. p. 46, in which Ariosto and Tasso are praised above Homer. For his former neglect of the Italian poets Voltaire had been taken to task by Rolli, the Italian translator of Milton.[72] The revised opinion of Voltaire, Warton says, "is very different from what formerly appeared in England."[73]

Warton's chief objections to Voltaire are naturally on religious grounds. For the same reason he catalogues at first Garth, who ridiculed the clergy, as merely "one of the freethinking WITS at Button's." This is also dropped in the final revision.[74]

The doubtful statement that "Lord Bolingbroke learned Spanish in less than three weeks" is rightly cancelled from the second volume.[75] Good taste also revised away a painfully fulsome compliment to the Speaker of the House of Commons.[76]

We have a few instances of progressive modification, a

[69] II (1st ed.), 36 n. Here Warton confuses Dion, the 1st century Greek orator and rhetorician and John Secundus, the 4th century Church Father. Both men were surnamed Chrysostom or "Golden mouthed" for their eloquence. It is Dion whom Warton somewhat carelessly quotes. Cf. the edition of Dion [or Dio] by J. de Arnim, II, p. 253 (1893). Oratio [Essay] XVIII, 8.
[70] I (4th ed.), 386. [72] I (4th ed.), 385 n.
[71] II (4th ed.), 403 n. [73] I (4th ed.), 138 n.
[74] I (3rd ed.), 222; (4th ed.), 224.
[75] (1st ed.), p. 83 n.; (4th ed.), p. 20 n.
[76] II (1st ed.), 98 n.; (4th ed.), 36 n.

little of each in the three revisions. He said that the most excellent of Dryden's prologues were "written on occasion of the players going to Oxford." He then lamented the decline of this custom, saying that no good reason could be assigned for it, unless it were that the players had followed the "cant of decrying that most learned university." In 1772 this accusation against the players vanishes and is replaced by a compliment to Dr. Ralph Bathurst, who had instituted the custom of the plays while he was vice-chancellor of the university. In 1782 the phrase deploring the abandonment of the plays is also dropped.[77] In 1756 and '62 he quotes four rather long paragraphs from Johnson's *Rambler* on the systems and authority of critics. In 1772 one is dropped, and in 1782 two more are, leaving finally only one short remark.[78]

A striking instance of these changes due to growth of taste and judgment occurs in Volume Two where Warton at first condemned the close of Gray's *The Bard*. In the revision later in the year he corrects his error—"On more closely and attentively considering the subject, I am inclined to alter my opinion, concerning the conclusion of this fine Ode of Mr. Gray." He then gives an enthusiastic appreciation of the ode, justifying the poet fully.[79] The criticism occurs in the portion of Volume Two printed "above twenty years ago" and as first set down is evidently a young critic's hasty judgment. The change is illustrative of Warton's steady growth in romantic taste and his boldness in expressing it.

An instance showing Warton's response to growing scholarship is found in this: in 1756 he had a passage on the origin of the story of Palamon and Arcite. He said that it was in existence before "Boccace's time and that some had ascribed it

---

[77] I (2nd ed.), 257; (3rd ed.), 266 f.; (4th ed.), 269.
[78] I (2nd ed.), 121-24; (3rd ed.), 125-27; (4th ed.), 126.
[79] II (1st ed.), 43; I (4th ed.), 394 n. He proceeds with a full page of analysis and justification of *The Bard*.

AN

ESSAY

ON THE

GENIUS AND WRITINGS

OF

POPE.

IN TWO VOLUMES.

By *JOSEPH WARTON, D. D.*

VOL. I.

THE FIFTH EDITION, CORRECTED.

To which is now added,

AN INDEX.

Satyra quidem tota nostra est: in qua primus insignem laudem adeptus est Lucilius; qui quosdam ita deditos sibi adhuc habet amatores, ut eum, non ejusdem modo operis autoribus, sed omnibus poetis, præferre non dubitent.
QUINTILIAN.

LONDON:

Printed by Thomas Maiden, Sherbourn-Lane, Lombard-Street,

FOR W J. AND J. RICHARDSON; OTRIDGE AND SON; J. WALKER; CUTHELL AND MARTIN; R. FAULDER; R LEA; OGILVY AND SON; J. NUNN; E. JEFFERY; LACKINGTON, ALLEN, AND CO. LONGMAN, HURST, REES, AND ORME; CADELL AND DAVIES; J. AND A. ARCH; J. ASPERNE; AND VERNOR, HOOD, AND SHARPE.

1806.

Title-page of the fifth edition of Joseph Warton's "*An Essay on . . . Pope,*" Volume I, *1806*.

"to a writer almost unknown, called Alanus de Insulis." This passage, like that on *The Bard*, is in the matter printed before 1762. But Warton has kept up with Tyrwhitt's work on Chaucer, published in 1775, and so when he gets a chance to correct this long-since printed matter, he gives Tyrwhitt's conclusions as to Chaucer's indebtedness to Boccaccio.[80]

(f) In some cases Warton's reading served only to make uncertain his previous sureness. In 1756 he was quite dogmatically certain that Addison used all his arts to suppress the rising merits of Pope and gave five specifications in his accusation. He stated that Addison's behavior extorted from Pope his famous "character" of Atticus.[81] This dictum of Warton's remains in the second and third editions. But in 1782, while the accusations are kept, they are reduced to hearsay, suppositions, reports—"if we can credit the reports," "it is asserted," "this usage supposed. . . ."[82] He had evidently read and could not but reflect Blackstone's celebrated defense of Addison, published in 1778.[83] Though he would not yield completely, he could not remain "certain." Up to 1772 he said that the second age of the world's great blooming "has never yet been sufficiently taken notice of." In 1782 this is softened to "seems not to have been, etc."[84] In the same way *"The Henriade* is free from any very gross faults" becomes "Tho' *the Henriade* should be allowed to be, etc."[85]

At first he was sure he had a piece of new, even startling, information—that the English Alexandrine measure was not

[80] II (1st ed.), 5 f.; I (4th ed.), 352 ff.
[81] See *Epistle to Dr. Arbuthnot*, ll. 193 ff.
[82] I (3rd ed.), 159 f.; (4th ed.), 158 f.
[83] See Andrew Kippis and others, *Biographia Britannica; or, the Lives of the Most Eminent Persons Who Have Flourished in Great Britain and Ireland, from the Earliest Ages, to the Present Times.* . . . (2nd ed., London, 1778-93), I (1778), 56-58. Cf. *Essay*, II (4th ed.), 242 ff.
[84] I (3rd and 4th edd.), 190.
[85] I (3rd ed.), 206 f.; (4th ed.), 207 f.

CHANGES MADE IN THE FIVE EDITIONS

modern, as supposed, but was used ("with the addition of two syllables"!) by Robert of Gloucester, Warner, and Drayton, and that "Dryden was the first who introduced it in our English heroic." But in his first revision all reference to Robert and the Elizabethans disappeared, and Dryden was left as "the first who introduced this measure into our English heroic." In the third edition he becomes still more cautious and ventures only that Dryden "introduced the frequent use of this measure."[86] He thus saves his face by dodging. Of course he was on the right track at first and should have merely deepened his knowledge.[87]

(g) We next have a few changes in the nature of additions of reasons and explanations for his critical judgments—all seemingly due to this growth of his information and culture. In the first edition we have the statement that "unvaried rhymes highly disgust readers of a good ear." When he revises six years later he adds two reasons for his judgment,— that such rhymes lack novelty, and that they imply carelessness and laziness on the part of the poet.[88] We have one instance in which an explanation of his reasons for inserting a stanza from an ode by Gilbert West is withdrawn because of an evident exaggeration.[89] Under this head are a large number of miscellaneous enlargements which do not affect the substance of his remarks. They are in each instance a few words to make clear or strong what he has said—the chatty addenda of a scholar growing old. There are 4 in the second edition of Volume One, 13 in the third, and 6 in the fourth and 33 in Volume Two. A few are here cited as examples. To his observation that Dryden gave "a secret charm, and a natural

---

[86] I (1st ed.), 150; (2nd ed.), 147; (3rd ed.), 151.
[87] See *English Verse Specimens Illustrating Its Principles and History* (ed. Raymond M. Alden, New York, 1903), pp. 252-59.
[88] I (1st ed.), 149; (2nd ed.), 146.
[89] I (1st ed.), 69 f.; (2nd ed.), 67. Cf. above, p. 60.

air to his verses" by the delicate introduction of common words, he adds in revision, "well knowing of what consequence it was sometimes to soften and subdue his tints, and not to paint and adorn every object he touched, with perpetual pomp and unremitted splendor."[90] Upon the mention of Gray's name the revision introduces an eight-line stanza, probably by Warton himself, in high praise of the poet. It is not relevant to the observations he is making.[91] The first edition of Volume Two says that Spence's *Essay on Pope's Odyssey* is "a work of the truest taste," the revision in the same year adds "and soundest criticism."[92] A just observation, notable in English criticism of Warton's day, on the greatness of "the native force of Cervantes's humour" is added in the same revision.[93]

(h) The last and most important of these modifications are those due to the notice Warton takes of happenings in the field of contemporary literature. They show that he took account of new work both in criticism and *belles-lettres*, that he grew in his taste for the new romantic work of Gray, Collins, Thomson, West, Akenside, and Young, and that he was aware of a movement about him which was creating new canons of criticism and furthering the decline of taste for Pope. They help to break the force of the common objection to criticism—that it takes notice of work only after it is well established in general approval, and that it cannot therefore adequately handle contemporary matters. Warton did not, of course, live to see the full significance of this new work nor to remake entirely his critical system derived so largely from the seventeenth century. He was a transition critic, but he was aware of the new things, tried to make a place for them, and can be asked for no handsomer appreciation of romantic work than his confident asser-

[90] II (1st ed.), 233 f.; (4th ed.), 175.
[91] II (1st ed.), 292; (4th ed.), 230 n.
[92] (1st ed.), p. 301; (4th ed.), p. 239.
[93] II (4th ed.), 404 n.

AN ESSAY
ON THE
GENIUS AND WRITINGS
OF
POPE.

IN TWO VOLUMES.

By *JOSEPH WARTON, D. D.*

VOL. II.

THE FIFTH EDITION, CORRECTED.

To which is now added,
AN INDEX.

Satyra quidem tota nostra est : in qua primus insignem laudem adeptus est Lucilius ; qui quosdam ita deditos sibi adhuc habet amatores, ut eum, non ejusdem modo operis autoribus, sed omnibus poetis, præferre non dubitent.
QUINTILIAN.

LONDON:
Printed by Thomas Maiden, Sherbourn-Lane, Lombard-Street,
FOR W. J. AND J. RICHARDSON; OTRIDGE AND SON; J. WALKER; CUTHELL AND MARTIN; R. FAULDER; R LEA; OGILVY AND SON; J. NUNN; E. JEFFERY; LACKINGTON, ALLEN, AND CO. LONGMAN, HURST, REES, AND ORME; CADELL AND DAVIES; J. AND A. ARCH J. ASPERNE; AND VERNOR, HOOD, AND SHARPE.

1806.

Title-page of the fifth edition of Joseph Warton's "An Essay on . . . Pope," Volume II, 1806.

tion that nothing in Pope equals in sublimity Gray's *Bard*.[94] There are some thirty-nine of these changes. A few are to avoid anachronisms. In the first issue there are, as pointed out above, many notices of publications and writers appearing "lately," "of late." Some of these are left even to the last edition, in order to give the time of composition and right credit, as when Warton says in 1762 that he hopes "some of the fair sex, of the abilities of Eloisa, (for we have two or three such at present in Great Britain,) will answer" Rousseau's "blasphemies against the passion of love."[95] This "at present" remains unchanged twenty years later in the fourth edition. Others, that made sharp inconsistency or would show failure to keep up with scholarship or which give personal credit for general opinions were altered, sometimes silently.

He takes note of, or quotes from, books published between his editions, as in 1762 of Hume's *Four Dissertations*, published in 1757.[96] Rousseau's *Discours sur l'origine & les fondemens de l'inégalité parmi les hommes* is quoted from the Amsterdam edition of 1755 in the first edition of the *Essay*.[97] It will be recalled that Warton's first volume appeared very early in the following year. Rousseau was, of course, immediately and widely read in England at this time. Gray's letters were published by Mason in 1775; Warton refers to them in the revision of 1782.[98] In 1756 he says he has "lately seen two or three lyric pieces, superior to any he [Pope] has left us"; he cites two of Akenside's and one of West's poems.[99] He is very tardy in recognizing Collins, but still in 1782 he includes both Collins and West in his list as having "strong and fruitful" imaginations.[100] We have seen

[94] II, 404 f.
[95] I (1st ed.), 308 n.; (4th ed.), 327 n.
[96] I (2nd ed.), 240 n.
[97] I, 309.
[98] I (4th ed.), 330 n.
[99] I (1st ed.), 69.
[100] I (4th ed.), 69 n.

CHANGES MADE IN THE FIVE EDITIONS 69

that Warton grew steadily in his appreciation of Gray. In the revision of Volume Two he adds Gray's poem on *Education and Government* to his list of great didactic poems, and regrets that Gray did not finish it.[101] This was first published by Mason in 1775. Bishop Law's translation of Bishop King's *Origin of Evil*, edition of 1781, is quoted the next year by Warton.[102] In the portion of Volume Two printed before 1762 and published in 1782, only Bacon, Hobbes, Prior, Addison, and Pope are given as English writers comparable with French authors in penetrating treatment of "life and manners." When he made his revision later in the year, Warton added the names of Richardson for his *Clarissa Harlowe* and Fielding for *Tom Jones*.[103] The second volume of Gibbon's *History of the Decline and Fall of the Roman Empire*, which appeared in 1781, is quoted by Warton the next year.[104] Reference has been made above[105] to Warton's prompt use of Tyrwhitt's essay on Chaucer, which appeared in 1775. In the first edition of Volume Two, in the part printed "above twenty years ago," he protested against the ignorance of the dramatic poets of Greece on the part of English poets and scholars. As soon as he can revise this, later in 1782, he adds this note: "When this was written the tragedies of Sophocles, Aeschylus, and Euripides, had not been translated:[106] nor had Mr. Mason published his Caractacus, nor Mr. Gray his Runic Odes, when page the 375th was written."[107]

Now Mason published *Caractacus* in 1759, a date impor-

---

[101] II (1st ed.), 119; (4th ed.), 58.
[102] II (1st ed.), 182 n.; (4th ed.), 125 n.
[103] II (1st ed.), 183 f.; (4th ed.), 126 f.
[104] II (4th ed.), 169 n.; cf. above, p. 52.
[105] See above, p. 64.
[106] He means of course in verse—see above, p. 19. In addition to those mentioned were R. Potter's translations of Aeschylus, in 1777, and of Euripides, in 1781.
[107] II (1st ed.), 30; I (4th ed.), 379 n.

tant in deciding that this section of his second volume (the one which was transferred to the first volume in the fourth edition) was written before that date. Gray's *Runic Odes* appeared in 1768. When he can modify his second volume, he inserts in an exclamation at the "dreadful images" of the *Edda* and the Runic poetry these words: "Such is Gray's *thrilling* Ode on the Descent of *Odin*."[108]

In the revision of 1762 he adds to his list of poems which show that all true genius did not die with Pope, poems of Thomson, Akenside, Young, Glover, and Gray. He specifies Gray's *Ode on a Distant Prospect of Eton College* and his "truly pathetic Monody on Lady Lyttleton."[109] These appeared in 1747. Horace Walpole's *Castle of Otranto* appeared in 1764. Warton makes a reference to this in 1782.[110] In 1756 he spoke of "the ingenious Mr. Dyer" as "this neglected author." Six years later the allegation of neglect has disappeared, probably because Warton found that many others also appreciated *Grongar Hill*.[111]

Taken together these references to recent publications are significant of Warton's care and make the *Essay* a valuable document in the history of eighteenth-century literature. Toward his great critical contemporary, Dr. Johnson, Warton is at first extremely deferential and full of praise. There is some change through the three issues, partly due to the lapse of time which makes reference to Johnson as "a recent writer" out of date, partly to a feeling that his early praise was too fulsome, partly to an actual change of critical attitudes. Johnson remained the steady champion of critical orthodoxy; Warton made many steps toward the new "romantic" positions.

[108] II (1st ed.), 50 n.; I (4th ed.), 402 n.
[109] I (1st ed.), 141; (2nd ed.), 138.
[110] II (1st ed.), 50 n.
[111] I (1st ed.), 35; (2nd ed.), 34 f.

APPENDICES

BIOGRAPHICAL NOTE

Joseph Warton was born at Dunsfold, Surrey, about April 22, 1722, the first of the three children of the Reverend Thomas Warton (1688-1745), who was graduated at Oxford in 1710 and was Professor of Poetry there from 1718 to 1728. He was also the vicar of Basingstoke, Hampshire, and master of the Grammar School there from 1728 to 1745. Joseph's brother, Thomas Warton, Jr., was also a graduate of Oxford and also Professor of Poetry there, from 1757 to 1767. He added greatly to his family's name by his poetry, but more particularly as critic, historian of English poetry, and Poet-Laureate.

Joseph was trained in his father's school at Basingstoke till he became, in 1736, a scholar in Winchester College, where he won some reputation as a student and poet of considerable parts. When he went up to Oxford, there was no vacancy at New College, the traditional home of Winchester boys; so he entered Oriel College. Here he continued his enthusiastic study of the classics and increased his reputation by the writing of poetry.

He was graduated in March, 1743, at once took holy orders, and became his father's curate at Basingstoke. In 1748 he became rector of Winslade. His patron, the Duke of Bolton, in 1751 invited Joseph to accompany him on a trip to the south of France. In 1755 he became usher, or second master, at Winchester College, and head master there in 1766, remaining till 1793. He proceeded at Oxford to the accumulated degrees of Bachelor and Doctor of Divinity in 1768. During these later years he was often in London with Dr. Johnson and his coterie of friends and in 1773 was made a member of the famous "Club."

In 1782 he was made a prebendary of St. Paul's by Bishop Lowth and in the next year was given the living of Chorley, which he soon exchanged for that of Wickham. He received, in 1788, a prebend at Winchester Cathedral and two years later the living at Easton, which was exchanged soon after for that of Upham.

Winchester College prospered greatly in the early years of Warton's head mastership, but he was a gentle, easy-going man, literary rather than scholarly, weak as a disciplinarian and administrator. During the later years of his régime there were frequent disorders and revolts among the students. After an especially fierce outbreak in 1793, Warton resigned and retired to Wickham.

In 1790 the death of his beloved brother, Thomas, who had been, for half a century, a sympathetic fellow student, broke Warton's spirit severely. He died February 23, 1800, and was buried in the north aisle of Winchester Cathedral. The Wykemites placed a beautiful monument by Flaxman to his honor in the south aisle of the Cathedral. There is a good portrait of him at New College, Oxford.

A List of Warton's Literary Works

1739 *Sappho's Advice*, in the *Gentleman's Magazine*, IX (October, 1739), 545. Published over name, "Monitorias," identified by his name in the margin. See Wooll's *Memoirs*, p. 107.

1742 *Fashion, An Epistolary Satire*, anonymous. Reprinted in Dodsley's *Collection of Poems* (1748), II, 547.

1744 *Ranelagh House*, a satire in prose.

1744 *The Enthusiast* and *The Dying Indian* (written in 1742 while an undergraduate at Oxford).

APPENDICES

1746 *Odes on Various Subjects*, with an important preface.
1746 *Superstition, an Ode*, in Dodsley's *Museum*, I (April, 1746), 55 f.
1748 With his sister Jane he published his father's *Poems on Several Occasions*.[1] For this volume each wrote an introductory ode, and Warton included his *An American Love Ode*.
1749 Issued a volume of his poems containing as fresh work his *Ode on Reading West's "Pindar"* and a Latin translation of his *Ode to Evening*.
1753 Edited *The Works of Virgil*, translating the Eclogues and Georgics but using Pitt's translation of the *Aeneid*. For this edition he wrote essays on pastoral, didactic, and epic poetry, and a life of Virgil, with notes for the whole. It was published in four volumes.
1753-56 Contributed twenty-four essays to Johnson's periodical, *The Adventurer;* these were chiefly literary criticism; contributed one essay on *Simplicity of Taste* to *The World*.
1756 *An Essay on the Writings and Genius of Pope*. Subsequent editions in 1762, 1772, and 1782 are traced in this monograph.
1758 Issued a second edition of *The Works of Virgil*.
1760 Worked at an edition of Theocritus but did not complete it.
1769 Warburton's edition of *The Works of Alexander Pope*, Vol. VI, contained notes by Warton and others.
1773 Planned and worked at *A History of the Revival of Learning*, conceived of while working at his edition of Virgil in 1753, but it was left unfinished.
1784 Announced *A History of Grecian, Roman, Italian, and French Poetry*, but it was never finished.

[1] Reproduced by the Facsimile Text Society, New York, 1930.

1787 Edited Sir Philip Sidney's *Defense of Poesie*.
1797 Issued an edition, in nine volumes, of the Works of Pope, with notes and essays on the types of poetry.

Bibliographical Note.—The best accounts of Warton and his work are: *Biographical Memoirs of the Late Rev. Joseph Warton, D.D.*, by John Wooll, London, 1806, and *Wykehamica, a History of Winchester College and Commoners from the Foundation to the Present Day*, by Henry C. Adams (London, 1878), pp. 134-53. An important note on Warton's life by Herbert Chitty, keeper of the Archives of Winchester College, appeared August 13, 1931, in the *Hampshire Chronicle* at Winchester. There are other significant books as to Winchester College, with rich accounts of Warton: *Winchester College, 1393-1893*, by Old Wykehamists, London, 1893; A. K. Cook, *Winchester College*, London, 1917; *Winchester College*, by the members of Winchester College Archeological Society, published by P. & G. Wells, Winchester, 1926.

www.ingramcontent.com/pod-product-compliance
Lightning Source LLC
Chambersburg PA
CBHW020754230426
43665CB00009B/589